14 Days

Y0-CQI-935

WITHDRAWN

QUEENS OF THE COURT
George Sullivan

Women's professional tennis has recently won identity and recognition as an exciting professional sport. Crowds are jamming arenas everywhere to watch the women play—and that never happened before.

One reason for the change is the type of tennis women play. It's more tactical and therefore more dramatic than the hard-hitting version men play. A second factor is the women themselves. There's dynamic Billie Jean King, the No. 1 American player in recent years, and overpowering Margaret Court, who achieved a rare tennis Grand Slam in 1970. There's relentless Chris Evert and the charming Evonne Goolagong, both perennial favorites of the fans. There's the diminutive Rosemary Casals and steely Virginia Wade.

These are the tennis "queens" profiled here—personal qualities that led to stardom, critical moments in their careers, their playing styles and court attitudes, plus the tournament records of each. The book also tells briefly of some outstanding women tennis stars of the past—Maureen Connolly, Alice Marble, and Althea Gibson among them. Illustrated with photographs.

QUEENS OF THE COURT

QUEENS OF THE COURT

George Sullivan

ILLUSTRATED WITH PHOTOGRAPHS

DODD, MEAD & COMPANY • New York

Acknowledgments

Many people were helpful and cooperative in the preparation of this book. Special thanks are offered: Pret Hadley, Public Relations. U. S. Lawn Tennis Association; Michael Ross, News and Information Bureau, Australian Consulate General; and Gary Wagner, Wagner-International Photos.

PICTURE CREDITS

Australian News & Information Bureau, 14, 16, 27; British Tourist Authority, 97; Pepsi Cola Mobile Tennis, 103; Timothy Sullivan, 12, 19, 31, 93, 95; United States Lawn Tennis Association, 100, 101, 104; Virginia Slims, 29, 55, 89. All other photographs are by George Sullivan.

Frontispiece: Billie Jean King, queen of American tennis.

CONTENTS

INTRODUCTION

Up until the 1970s, tournament tennis was a man's world almost exclusively. The men got the most prize money and virtually all the press coverage. The women's tournaments that were scheduled were kind of throw-ins. When you paid to see the men play, you were given the women at no additional charge.

All of this has changed remarkably. Women's tennis now has its own identity as an exciting professional sport.

Australia's Margaret Court can tell you about the changes that have taken place. She banked more than $200,000 in tournament earnings in 1973, making her one of the highest paid athletes in the world.

Or ask Billie Jean King. When she captured the U.S. Singles title at Forest Hills in 1967, the account of her triumph rated only three paragraphs in *The New York Times*. But today Billie Jean has to hide out from the press occasionally so she can concentrate on her game. And her popularity is such that she employs a full-time secretary, one of whose duties is to follow her employer around at tournaments and distribute slips of paper bearing Billie Jean's autograph to those who ask for it.

What brought about this metamorphosis? Part of what happened is a reflection of what happened to sports—participation sports, in particular—during the 1960s. Early in the decade, under the encouragement of the late President John F. Kennedy, the country was swept with a sudden awareness of physical fitness. Tennis' surge in popularity began at that time.

The early 1960s was also the period when promoters began putting important money into tennis in an effort to make it a big-time professional sport. Another factor was the revision of certain century-old tennis rules and regulations, particularly some of those that related to scoring and attire.

Tennis also took a giant step forward in 1968 when the championships at Wimbledon in England and the U.S. Nationals at Forest Hills went "open," meaning that professionals were allowed to compete in these tournaments along with amateurs. The following year the United States Lawn Tennis Association (USLTA) allowed nonprofessional players to accept prize money, another breakthrough.

These changes, however, did not have a profound effect upon women's professional tennis. As late as 1970, women were sometimes made to compete for one-tenth the prize money offered men players. Women's matches at major tournaments were given short shrift, often scheduled at early-morning hours on remote field courts. And daily newspapers gave about as much space to the women as they did to college water polo.

The women revolted. They did so by banding

Placard on display at Forest Hills in 1973 proclaimed the advances made by women's tennis.

together to organize and promote their own tournaments under the aegis of Gladys Heldman, publisher of *World Tennis* Magazine. Houston was the scene of the first women's tournament. It drew standing-room-only crowds.

That year, 1970, the total amount of prize money offered to women professionals wasn't much more than $50,000. But by 1972, women's prizes had zoomed to over half a million dollars, and the total exceeded a million dollars in 1973 and 1974. A cigarette company, Virginia Slims, was the tour's chief sponsor.

Women professionals are quick to admit that male players, being physically stronger, are superior in tennis. They hit the ball harder and run faster. From the standpoint of entertainment, however, this often works to their disadvantage. On grass or any other fast surface men's tennis often winds up being a service duel. Any given point is likely to be won by whoever is serving. If a player should happen to lose his service once, he's likely to lose the set.

Not so with women's tennis. It's much more tactical. Billie Jean King recalls a game against Australia's Kerry Melville during a tournament in San Francisco in 1972. In one exchange, with the two women scrambling back and forth over the length and breadth of the court, the ball crossed the net thirty-six times. When the point was finally decided, the crowd gave the pair a standing ovation. In other words, quite often the women put on a better show.

One other important factor in the success of women's tennis must be mentioned: the women themselves. There's the intimidating Billie Jean King, overpowering Margaret Court, relentless Chris Evert, mesmerizing Evonne Goolagong, acrobatic Rosie Casals, and steely Virginia Wade. Anyone who has ever seen them on the courts has a clear understanding of why women's tennis has come so far so fast.

QUEENS OF THE COURT

GRAND SLAMMER:
Margaret Court

"She may be the greatest of all time."

That's what people say about Margaret Court, the tall, strong Australian who has won more major tennis titles than any other woman in the history of the game. She can't remember exactly how many herself, but as of January, 1974, the number was twenty-four.

Margaret ranks as one of the two women players to have scored a Grand Slam, sweeping the Australian Open, the French Open, the All-England championship at Wimbledon, and the U.S. Open at Forest Hills, all in the same year, 1970.

A friendly person, with short brown hair and soft blue eyes, Margaret used to be terribly shy. She is much less so now, but prefers the company of Australian friends rather than the casual acquaintances she makes as a touring professional. She speaks in a small voice, the words colored by an amiable Australian accent. Friends are addressed as "luv." "Player" is pronounced "plier." "How's it going?" is "Ow-zit gun?"

Women's lib is not for Margaret. She married yachtsman Barry Court in 1967, and he is never far from her side. Their first child, a boy, was born in 1972. Named Danny, he traveled with the Courts everywhere they went.

Margaret Court sizes up her opponent.

Margaret is marvelously equipped physically to play tennis. A big-boned woman, she stands 5-foot-9 and weighs 150 pounds. Her serve is hard and fast. Her forehand shots are struck with awesome power. Her backhand strokes have style and finesse. Like all great champions, she has an instinct for volleying and, because of her long arms, is difficult to pass once she gets to the net. She covers the court beautifully and has the stamina of a long-distance runner.

What's it like to play against Margaret Court?

"She frightens you when you look at her from the other side of the court," says Rosemary Casals. "She seems to be all arms and legs. You can't get the ball out of her reach."

"She simply overpowers most opponents," says Billie Jean King. "You have to get on top of her at the start and never let her get away. If she breaks on top, her confidence soars and she is murderous."

Margaret has been a major force in women's tennis since 1960, when, at the age of seventeen, she won the Australian Open, her first major triumph. But maintaining her eminence has been no easy task for Margaret. At random times during her career, she has been struck with attacks of nervousness. Sometimes these center-court jitters have cost her matches, even tournaments. But it is a measure of her pride and will to win that more often than not she has been able to regain control and steer her way to victory.

Australia is a big country, about as big as the

Her range and reach make Margaret a formidable opponent.

United States, if you don't count Alaska. But it is not very populous. About 12,500,000 people live there, approximately the same number as live in the state of Pennsylvania.

If you ever visited the country, you would probably come away with the impression that every one of the inhabitants plays tennis, or at least follows the game. It's true. Tennis is Australia's national sport.

A chief reason for the game's popularity is the Australian climate. It is seldom cold. Snow is to be seen only in the mountains. This means that tennis can be played throughout the year.

But it is not just because of the agreeable climate that so many outstanding tennis players come out of Australia. Much credit has to go to the thousands of people who work on a voluntary basis as coaches and in the promotion of junior tournaments. Even the smallest hamlet has its tennis committee.

In addition, each one of the six Australian states has its own tennis association, and each of these associations conducts tournaments for boys and girls in various age groups. Any youngster with more than average ability is watched carefully, entered into state-wide competition, and given special instruction by prominent coaches.

This was the path that Margaret followed. She was born Margaret Smith on July 16, 1942, in Albury, a small town in the state of New South Wales about two hundred miles north of Melbourne. Her father was a foreman for a dairy products plant.

The youngest of four children—two boys and two girls—Margaret was good in all sports, including basketball, softball, and track. As for tennis, well, everyone played tennis. It was part of growing up.

Across the street from the modest Smith home were the fine grass courts of the Albury and Border Lawn Tennis Association. Margaret could stand in her front yard and throw a tennis ball onto center court.

As children, Margaret and her friends, all boys, weren't permitted to use the courts, so they would sneak through a hole in the high fence that surrounded the club, and play until they were spotted by Wal Rutter, the club professional, and chased away. They found that whenever they used one particular back court, a tall, thick hedge screened them from Mr. Rutter's view, provided that the player at one end of the court stayed at the net.

It was at the net that the boys posted Margaret. She couldn't permit herself to miss, because if she did and had to retrieve the ball, she risked being spotted by Mr. Rutter. "That's how I learned to volley," Margaret now says.

Margaret began tennis as a left-hander, but the boys ridiculed her about playing from that side. "There was never a good left-handed player," she was told. To stop the teasing, Margaret switched over to her right hand.

When she was ten, Margaret and her friends enrolled in a Saturday morning tennis clinic at the

Margaret at twenty-one during a state championship in Australia.

Albury courts. "I remember that I could beat most of the boys in the class and certainly the girls," says Margaret in her biography, *The Margaret Smith Story*. "Some of the girls would complain to Mr. Rutter because I hit the ball too hard."

The instructors at the club, realizing her talent, used Margaret to show the other students how to execute the various strokes. She would be brought up to the front of the class, sometimes as large as two hundred children, and as the instructor said, "This is the way to hit a backhand shot," Margaret would demonstrate. She continued as a star pupil for three years. It gave her confidence in herself and made her think that perhaps she could become something important in tennis.

At the end of the coaching season, Mr. Rutter and his wife would organize championship competition among the students. Margaret won her age division for four straight years.

She kept right on winning after she had advanced to the senior division. By the time she was fifteen, she had won most of the events in the country districts of Victoria and New South Wales, and the Smith home was bursting with trophies, more than sixty of them. Tennis now completely absorbed her. She practically lived on the courts. She recalls she "hated" schoolwork, mostly because it required time she could be devoting to tennis.

She served with enormous power for a teen-ager

and her groundstrokes were almost flawless. Because she beat other teen-agers so easily, she sought out adult competition. When Mr. Rutter was too busy to play, she'd often help him with his chores so he could finish ahead of time. She painted net posts, marked the courts, and learned to drive the big power mower used to keep the grass trimmed. Other times, Margaret would wait for local businessmen to come to the courts after work and then ask them "to give her a hit."

Margaret's game kept improving, and in the summer of 1958 and 1959 she reached the finals of both the Victorian and Australian junior championships, only to lose to a former schoolgirl opponent named Jan Lehane. "You will not get anywhere in the world until you beat that girl," Mr. Rutter told her. "You will have to try harder."

One day Mr. Rutter spoke to Frank Sedgman, an Australian tennis great of the early 1950's, about Margaret, telling him of her great potential. Sedgman became interested in her, and after watching her in a tryout suggested that she move to Melbourne where he could coach her. The idea thrilled Margaret. Her sister June had a flat in Auburn, a Melbourne suburb, and Margaret would live with her.

Margaret has described herself as a "country bumpkin" at this stage of her life. She was very tall for her age, with spindly legs and arms. She was awkward and shy. She had never dated.

Margaret attacks off her forehand during a Federation Cup match in Australia.

Once settled in Melbourne, Margaret embarked on an intensive training program under Sedgman's direction. To strengthen her muscles, she lifted weights and worked with pulleys and dumbbells. One of her exercises was to swing a lead-weighted racket. Soon she began to develop powerful shoulders and arms, and her pipestem legs swelled with shapely calves and thighs. Each morning, no matter what the weather, she would sprint in a local park.

That winter in the Wilson Cup series of matches, in which the best Australian girls compete, Margaret defeated her old adversary, Jan Lehane. Margaret felt certain that she had passed an important milestone in her career.

When the Australian championships got under way in Brisbane early in 1960, Margaret was seeded No. 7. The No. 1 seed was Maria Bueno, the graceful Brazilian who had won both the Wimbledon and Forest Hills the year before. After winning her early-round matches, Margaret faced Maria in the finals. It was hot and humid as the match began but Margaret felt strong and fit. Nearly three thousand people watched, the biggest crowd that she had ever played before.

Margaret took the first set* 7-5, but tightened under the pressure to lose the second, 6-3. In the third and deciding set, Margaret broke Maria's serve to take a 3-1 lead, and then held on to make it 5-2.

* For a definition of this and other scoring terms, see page 105.

17

Margaret tunes up her big serve.

"Stay calm and hit the ball hard," she told herself.

Maria edged to within one point, 5-4, and her first serve in the tenth game was good. But Margaret lunged for the ball off her forehand and belted it back, and Maria could not reach it. Then Maria put a volley into the net to fall behind, 0-30.

After they each took a point, Maria stroked a volley that Margaret could not handle. Now Margaret led, 40-30. One more point was all she needed. As Margaret walked back to take the serve, she swept perspiration from her forehead with her index finger and tried to compose herself. In came Maria's serve. Margaret stepped into the ball and slammed it back wide to her rival's forehand. Maria stretched but the best she could do was punch the ball into the net. Margaret had won. She was—at seventeen—the Australian women's champion, the youngest player and first junior ever to win the championship.

"Good Lord!" declared Frank Sedgman when he received the news back in Melbourne. "I thought she had promise but I didn't expect anything like this so soon." The world of international tennis—Wimbledon, Forest Hills, and all the other important events—now beckoned.

To win at Wimbledon is the dream of every top-flight tennis player. Wimbledon is the site just outside London where the All-England championships are decided each year. It has been described as the greatest tennis show on earth. The first championship matches were held there in 1877.

"There's a flavor and a greatness about Wimbledon," Billie Jean King has said, "that puts it on a pedestal by itself." Part of Wimbledon's character is the majestic quality it has, the dignity and grandeur with which matches are conducted. This is especially true of the matches held on "center court," the single grass court enclosed by a huge covered amphitheatre.

Another important part of the Wimbledon mystique is the enthusiasm that all of England has for the matches. The throngs that attend the tournament include gentlemen in frock coats and top hats, and ladies in silks and ruffles. There are also thousands of secretaries, students, store clerks, and businessmen in attendance, most of them arriving by special trains run from London. Journalists from all parts of the world are on hand. The British press covers the matches with the same verve they devote to a royal wedding.

Margaret's first appearance at Wimbledon came in 1961. She did about as well as she hoped to do, reaching the quarterfinals. But when she returned in 1962, a lanky twenty-year-old, she was expected to offer a strong challenge for the title. Earlier in the year, she had won the Australian crown for the third time, and she had also collected championships in France and Italy. In recognition of all of these achievements, tournament officials seeded her No. 1.

"Murderous" is how one opponent described Margaret's powerful serve-and-volley game.

In the second round, Margaret was scheduled to meet a chunky, freckle-faced young American by the name of Billie Jean Moffitt. Beating Billie Jean would be only a formality, so everyone thought.

Margaret won the first set with ease, but the bouncy Billie Jean surged back to capture the next two sets, sending Margaret down to a crushing defeat. When the match was over, Margaret buried her face in a towel at the umpire's chair and fought hard to control herself. It marked the first time in the history of Wimbledon that a top-seeded player had failed to win a match.

It did not take Margaret long to shake off the shock of what happened at Wimbledon. She arrived in the United States that summer filled with a determination to regain the form that had carried her to the championships of France and Italy earlier in the year.

She was magnificent at Forest Hills, reaching the finals where she faced the powerful Darlene Hard, the champion in both 1960 and 1961. Margaret took the first set, 9-7, and she was leading in the second set, 4-2, when she came close to being victimized by what she felt to be an extraordinary bit of gamesmanship.

Darlene struck a shot that went over the base line, which the linesman called "out." Darlene was obviously upset by the call. A few points later, Darlene hit a shot down the sideline, which by Margaret's reckoning was out by at least four inches.

When the linesman called "out," Darlene screamed back, "It was in!" Glaring at the linesman, Darlene walked toward the back of the court, then abruptly put her head in her hands and began to sob loudly. While thousands of spectators watched, she cried and cried.

Margaret had never seen anything to compare with this, and she didn't know what to do. She felt certain that the call had been right. She sat down on the court and waited for Darlene to stop.

The incident so rattled Margaret that when play resumed she found it difficult to concentrate and her lead melted away. But with the score 4-4, Margaret regained her touch, held her serve to go ahead, then broke Darlene's serve to win the set and match.

Margaret was thus able to return home with her head high, as the first Australian woman ever to win the singles championships of France, Italy, and America in the same year.

When Margaret arrived at Wimbledon the next year, the awful defeat that she had suffered at the hands of Billie Jean was still vivid in her memory. This time Margaret played the kind of tennis she was capable of, reaching the finals. Ironically, so did Billie Jean.

Margaret knew what people were saying about her, that the presence of Billie Jean and the importance of the match were going to make her jittery. The newspapers in London were full of stories saying that Margaret couldn't adjust to big-time tennis, that she cracked under pressure.

The match was delayed for two days because of heavy rain, which served to increase the tension. But when it finally got underway, it seemed that Billie Jean was the one with the jitters. She double-faulted three times in the opening game.

Margaret produced a series of crackling serves and deft volleys to earn a quick victory in the first set, 6-3, and forge ahead, 4-0, in the second set. At this point, Billie Jean started fighting back. She broke Margaret's serve and held her own to make the score 4-2. The crowd buzzed. Was Margaret beginning to crack?

"Take it easy," Margaret told herself, as she prepared to serve. "Take your time and keep your head." She took the game to build her lead to 5-2.

But Billie Jean was not finished. She held her serve and then broke Margaret's to creep within one point, 5-4.

Now Billie Jean served. Margaret's first return was a rifle shot that Billie Jean could not handle. Quickly, Margaret led, 40-15. The title was within her grasp.

At 40-30, Margaret slammed a backhand down the line that Billie Jean could not possibly reach, and as Margaret watched it skim over the net she said to herself, "Please, Lord, let it go in." She waited for the linesman to say something. When he didn't, Margaret knew that she was the Wimbledon champion at last.

There was no prancing or jumping for joy. Instead of exhilaration, Margaret felt relief as the pressure

Awaiting a serve, Margaret bends deeply from the waist; her feet are wide apart.

that she had carried for so many months drained away.

Billie Jean came over to the net to shake hands. "I thought that would happen," she said. "You were just too good."

Margaret stunned the world of tennis in 1966 with the announcement that she was quitting the game. "I'm tired of traveling," she said, "of packing and unpacking suitcases all the time. I'm tired of chasing tennis balls." She didn't touch a tennis racket for sixteen months, although she kept in condition by playing squash, a racket game played with a hard rubber ball on a walled court.

Margaret opened a boutique called The Peephole, in Perth, the beautiful capital of Western Australia. There she met a tall and friendly wool broker and yachtsman named Barry Court. They were married in October, 1967.

Margaret started playing tennis again with her husband and their friends. "I started to enjoy it once more," she said, "and I got back into doing a lot of roadwork and hitting the courts regularly." She began entering tournaments and making her opponents wish that she had stayed retired. Before long, she was the No. 1 player in the world once more.

After Margaret had won the Australian Open in 1970, the ninth time she had captured the title, she set as her goal to score a Grand Slam. That meant she would have to win the French, British, and U.S. titles in the same year. Only once before had a woman

Practice session

player completed a Grand Slam. That was in 1953 when Maureen Connolly turned the trick.

Under a blue sky and burning sun, Margaret beat German's Helga Niessen to win the French Open, 6-2, 6-4. It was a much more difficult match than the score indicates. Helga, one of the most consistent players on the tour that summer, had Margaret on the run in the early stages. At 4-all in the second set, it began to look as if Margaret would not be able to maintain the pace much longer. But it was Helga who weakened, her forehand betraying her. Margaret thus took a giant step on the road to the Slam.

At Wimbledon, Margaret was crisply efficient in the early rounds, winning with relative ease. But she met resistance in the quarterfinals, again in the person of Helga Niessen, the German girl who had been troublesome in Paris.

As tall as Margaret and extremely graceful, Helga had seldom played on grass. To compensate for her lack of experience, she decided to change her style, attacking the net at the slightest opportunity.

Margaret, by running, stretching, and scrapping desperately, managed to ease ahead, 6-5. But Helga wouldn't relent, as she kept Margaret chasing her sharp-angled volleys. In the thirteenth game, Margaret lunged for a ball, fell heavily, then winced in pain. She had wrenched her ankle. Play was interrupted while the ankle was taped. When the girls resumed, poor Margaret double-faulted to lose the set.

The crowd was quiet and apprehensive as the second set began. Many spectators believed they were about to see a great champion eliminated. But Margaret was determined not to give up without a fight. She stopped making mistakes and forgot about her injured ankle. The first game was hard fought but Margaret won. The same thing happened in the second game. Then Helga's challenge began to fade, and Margaret roared to a superb victory, 6-0. The third set was almost a replay of the second, Margaret winning again, 6-0.

Margaret was to meet Rosemary Casals in the semifinals, but she was more concerned about her sore ankle than the fiery Rosie. To give the ankle as much rest as possible, Margaret withdrew from the doubles and mixed doubles events.

Margaret took a 4-1 lead, but Rosemary, serving three perfect aces, and drawing ooh's and aah's from the crowd for her seemingly impossible returns, drew even at 4-all. It was Margaret's serve. Rosie was as shrewd as she had ever been, using drop shots and lobs to go ahead, 40-15. If there ever was a time for Margaret to become tense and fail, this was it. But she did not. Moving about the court with surprising ease, and showing not the slightest bit of tension, Margaret answered Rosie's challenge with an attack of her own, taking the crucial ninth game to edge into the lead, 5-4. Rosemary's resistance began to melt soon after. Margaret took the set, 6-4. The second set lasted only seventeen minutes. Margaret won, 6-1.

23

The final match, with Margaret opposing Billie Jean King, produced some of the finest tennis Wimbledon has ever seen. Both women were magnificent, dazzling the crowd with their powerful serves and volleying skill. If Margaret's ankle pained her, she did not show it.

In the early stages of the first set, Billie Jean seemed to have the upper hand. Three times she served at set point, but each time Margaret was able to turn aside the challenge. At 12-11, Margaret had her first set point, but a glorious drop shot by Billie Jean saved the day. At 13-12, Margaret got another chance. Billie Jean's serve was hard and true, but Margaret rifled the ball back with a magnificent crosscourt backhand, and Billie Jean could not handle it.

Margaret seemed much more in control in the second set. Billie Jean hung on, fighting back with perfect drop shots whenever she was on the brink of elimination. Margaret reached match point at 9-8, but could not close the door. Four more times Margaret had Billie Jean at match point, and each time Billie Jean resisted.

The crowd was hushed and expectant. Margaret gritted her teeth. Finally, in the seventeenth game, Margaret passed Billie Jean with a torrid backhand drive and the American netted it, giving Margaret the match.

Opposite: *Autograph session*

The crowd responded with a tremendous ovation. Margaret now needed only the U.S. title to become the second woman in history to achieve a Grand Slam.

Margaret breezed through the early rounds at Forest Hills, hardly being tested. "The Australian is so far ahead of the other girls and her matches are so one-sided that it is difficult to judge how great she is," *World Tennis* Magazine would say in its account of the tournament.

Margaret did encounter some resistance in the semifinals, when she faced Nancy Richey. Nancy managed to break Margaret's serve, the first time it had happened during the tournament, and she made Margaret do plenty of running. Though Margaret won, 6-1, 6-3, it was a difficult match.

Now, only Rosie Casals stood in the way of the championship and the Grand Slam. Not only was the match of critical importance to Margaret, but it was to Rosie, too. Only twenty-two years old, Rosemary Casals had blossomed suddenly in 1966, making the quarterfinals at Wimbledon, and since that time she had come to be regarded as one of the world's best players. But this was the first time she had reached the finals in a major tournament. Winning it was crucial to her and her career.

Both women were indecisive as the match opened. Margaret's forehand lacked its usual authority and she seemed hesitant about taking the net. But Rosie wasn't able to take advantage of Margaret's lapses,

Off her backhand, Margaret hits with both power and finesse.

making one error after another. She lost her serve at 3-2 and again at 5-2 and, thus, the set went to Margaret, 6-2.

The win did nothing to bolster Margaret's confidence nor raise her level of play. With the score 1-1 in the second set, Rosie launched a determined attack, breaking Margaret's serve with hard to handle crosscourt returns. Margaret continued to hang back, and when she did move in she often put the ball in the net. She did not look like the world's No. 1 player. Rosie won the set, 6-2.

Margaret knew that she was facing disaster unless she could settle down. Her first serve cannonaded from her racket, and when the return was feeble, Margaret flashed to the net to put the point away. She passed Rosie with brilliant backhand shots and sent tantalizing lobs over her head. Margaret quickly led, 3-0. She now seemed unbeatable.

Within minutes it was 5-1, Margaret serving. Her first serve was unreturnable. So was her second. The next point Margaret won with a perfect lob, and then Rosie netted a forehand.

It was over. Margaret had won the U.S. Open and had scored the second women's Grand Slam in history. The crowd cheered her wildly. Her husband rushed up to congratulate her. "What was the first thing she said to you?" a reporter asked him later. "She said," he answered, "that she couldn't believe it."

Once she had achieved the Grand Slam, Margaret

thought that perhaps she had conquered her center-court jitters once and for all. But such wasn't the case. Her nerves got the best of her in the Wimbledon final the very next year. Playing against Evonne Goolagong, Margaret was tentative about moving and going to the net. Shots flew from her forehand haphazardly and she double-faulted frequently. It was not a pretty sight. She lost—naturally.

Not long after the tournament, Margaret announced that she was expecting a baby. There were no more tournaments that year. Margaret returned to the tournament trail after the baby was born. It didn't take her long to regain her championship form once more.

She seemed headed for the best season of her career in 1973. "I'm more relaxed this year," she told tennis writer Murray Janoff that spring. "I find I'm more secure as a person. I also feel I'm stronger. I've worked on my game. I'm as enthusiastic as ever."

But she was to be victimized by her nerves one more time. The scene was not Wimbledon nor Forest Hills, but an obscure country club in Ramona, California, about forty miles south of San Diego. And her opponent wasn't Billie Jean King or Rosemary Casals, but a fifty-five-year-old bespectacled and bowlegged former Wimbledon champion by the name of Bobby Riggs. The match in question, described by Riggs as the "Battle of the Sexes," was to cause as much commotion as any tennis happening in years.

Margaret plays a forehand volley during Australian singles match in Melbourne.

The contest had been launched many months before, when Riggs, weary of Billie Jean King's loud campaign for higher prize money for women players, challenged her to a match, putting up $5,000 as a reward if she could beat him. His selling point was that, at fifty-five, he should present no great problem to a woman of her consummate skills. But Billie, realizing that she had nothing to gain ($5,000 not being a sum that excited her), rejected the offer. Riggs then challenged Margaret Court and she accepted.

In his heyday, Riggs was perhaps the finest all-around player in the game. There was no shot that he could not make and his lob was said to be the deadliest of all time. But time had eroded his skills and dulled his reflexes. And there was an awful lot of time involved. The year he won at Wimbledon was 1939, three years before Margaret was born.

"If Bobby were younger, I think there would be no doubt who would win," said Pauline Betz Addie, who had won at Wimbledon herself. "The best man player can easily beat the best woman player." This fact is generally acknowledged. The powerful serve and volley game the men play by virtue of their physical superiority gives them an advantage over their women counterparts.

Mrs. Addie, noting that the years had sapped Riggs' speed and strength, added, "Margaret should win on sheer strength. She serves harder and she can hit the ball with greater force both from the backcourt and at the net."

While Riggs may have been a has-been as a player, as a hustler he was in his prime. To hustle, says the dictionary, means to induce someone to gamble in a game set up against him [or her]. In the parlance of the hustler, Margaret was the mark, the pigeon.

Several times she was warned about Riggs' hustling tricks. To rattle her, he was expected to resort to such tactics as taking extra time between serves, tossing up a ball to serve and not hitting it, or chattering endlessly during normal court breaks.

His mouth was a formidable weapon. From the day the match was first announced, Riggs never stopped talking. "Women's tennis? I think it stinks," he would say to anyone who would listen. "They hit the ball back and forth, have a lot of nice volleys, and you see some pretty legs. But it's night and day compared to men's tennis."

He described Margaret as being younger, stronger, bigger, and faster than he was. "She's got a better serve, a better volley, and a better overhead," he said. "She's got me beat in every department except, maybe, thinking, strategy, experience."

Riggs said this was to be the "Match of the Century." It seemed the media believed him. The press was filled with news stories of the match, and a television network agreed to beam the contest into living rooms throughout the United States and provide live satellite coverage to Australia and several other countries.

Margaret Court

Margaret, accompanied by her husband and son Danny, then fourteen months old, arrived at the site two days before the match. A swarm of newspaper reporters and photographers descended upon her. Riggs was amidst them. He tweaked Margaret on the cheek; Danny, too.

"Do you realize, Margaret, that this is the most important match you ever played?" said Riggs. "Just think how many women are counting on you."

Margaret didn't answer.

"Bill Talbert says he wants us to play a return match at Forest Hills for $20,000," Riggs continued. "Do you want to take him up on it?"

Margaret managed a weak smile. "Get off it, luv," she said.

Tennis is a serious business to Margaret. She didn't like all the furor. It was like being a part of a circus sideshow. It made her uncomfortable.

The day of the match was warm and sunny. Ironically, it happened to be Mother's Day. Margaret surprised many observers by wearing a pastel outfit of green and gold (the Australian colors). It was the first time she had ever worn anything but white for a match.

When the two met at the net, Riggs, in a blue shirt, white shorts, and wearing a visor, presented Margaret with a spray of red roses. Margaret smiled and curtsied.

Riggs won the toss and elected to serve. The ball came to Margaret's forehand, softly, slowly, in a big rainbow arc. Margaret plopped it into the net. That rather set the pattern for all that was to follow.

When she netted an overhead in the second game to fall behind, love-30, Margaret's confidence, precarious till then, seemed to wither completely. At courtside a friend of Margaret's turned to her husband. "Is she nervous?" she asked. "Really bad," he answered.

Instead of playing in her usual aggressive manner, Margaret let Riggs set the tempo. He threw her an assortment of slow spins, chops, lobs, and drop shots. Sometimes the pace was slower than you might expect to see at a weekend public-courts match. Margaret was unable to cope with it.

To Riggs' credit, it must be said that he played his shots with pinpoint control and accuracy, hitting them straight down the middle whenever he could, right into Margaret's power. The result was that Margaret had difficulty unwinding her long arms and getting her feet set. She seemed almost determined to beat herself. She stayed in the backcourt, seldom going to the net, making error after error after error. She failed on nineteen of thirty-seven first serves. Riggs won, 6-2, 6-1.

Margaret was very near to tears at the end. To her credit, she kept her composure and dignity.

"What happened?" the reporters who clustered around her wanted to know. "He hit slower than the girls," she sighed. "It threw me off my rhythm and I couldn't get it back."

Riggs had another explanation. "I had been told she could get jittery," he said, "so I kept impressing on her what an important match this was, much bigger than any Wimbledon. The whole thing was pressure."

To win at Forest Hills in 1973 was very important to Margaret, about as important as the year she slammed. She had begun the year impressively, downing Evonne Goolagong in both the finals of the Australian Open and the New South Wales Open. She came to the United States and joined the Virginia Slims tour. She began by whipping Kerry Melville in San Francisco and Nancy Richey Gunter in Los Angeles, then Kerry Melville again in Bethesda, Maryland. She was just warming up. Of the thirteen Virginia Slims tournaments she entered, Margaret won ten, plus over $75,000 in prize money.

Then came Mother's Day at Ramona, California. The humiliation she suffered at the hands of Bobby Riggs paled her earlier achievements. Wimbledon, where she fell victim to the youthful Chris Evert, had added to her discontent.

When she returned to the United States from England that summer, she decided that what she needed more than anything else was rest and relaxation. The family took a three-week vacation in the

Opposite: Margaret at the U.S. Open at Forest Hills in 1973, where she won her sixth singles title.

Florida Keys, Margaret's first real break that year. She tuned up for Forest Hills by entering the Virginia Slims tournament in Nashville, and there she defeated Billie Jean King in the finals.

The triumph and the vacation worked wonders. When she arrived at Forest Hills in mid-August, her confidence was restored. "I'm keen to win," she told interviewers. There was an added incentive in that the women's prize money was, for the first time, equal to that of the men's. Winning would be worth $25,000.

The early matches were played in withering heat, with temperatures shooting above ninety degrees for nine straight days. But it never seemed to bother Margaret. Even when she faced Virginia Wade in the quarterfinals, and the dark-haired English girl used her powerful serve-and-volley game to run her around the court, Margaret endured, winning in two sets. Margaret then whipped Chris Evert in their semifinal match, going to the net frequently in the decisive third set.

The weather cooled off for the finals and a crowd of 15,137—the largest in the history of Forest Hills —jammed into the great concrete horseshoe to watch Margaret duel Evonne Goolagong. It promised to be an exciting match. Margaret had the harder serve and a superior net game, while Evonne's strengths were her quicker reflexes and tremendous agility.

In the early stages, Evonne's penetrating serves neutralized Margaret's ability to rush the net. The younger woman got away to a 4-1 lead. Margaret, who has often said that she plays better when she's behind "because it makes me concentrate more," came rampaging back. Behind, 15-40, with it her serve, she managed to pull out the game.

"The way to win matches on grass is to get the first serve in," is an adage every tennis coach quotes. Well, Evonne started missing with her first serves, and any time she did, Margaret would return a spinning shot into the corner, sprint to the net, and then volley home a winner. The set went to Margaret, 7-6.

In the second set, Margaret seemed hesitant. Evonne took five of the last six games to even matters at a set apiece. Margaret knew what she had to do— be decisive, go to the net. When Evonne started failing with her first serve again, it paved the way for her. It ended quickly, Margaret winning, 6-2. It was her sixth U.S. Singles championship.

"She may be the greatest of all time."

That's what people were saying about Margaret after she scored her Grand Slam in 1970. They were saying it again after she won at Forest Hills in 1973.

With that kind of billing, and considering all that she has achieved, one would think that Margaret Court has run out of worlds to conquer. Not so. "I'd like to be the first woman to win the Grand Slam twice," she says. And there's that character named Bobby Riggs. More than anything else, Margaret would like to get another crack at him.

MARGARET COURT: Major Championship Records

U.S. Singles—1962, 1965, 1968, 1969, 1970, 1973
U.S. Doubles—1963 (with Robyn Ebbern); 1968 (with Maria Bueno); 1969 (with Virginia Wade); 1970 (with Judy Tegart Dalton)
U.S. Mixed Doubles—1961 (with Robert Mark); 1962, 1965 (with Fred Stolle); 1963 (with Ken Fletcher); 1964 (with John Newcombe); 1969, 1970 (with Marty Riessen)
Wimbledon Singles—1963, 1965, 1970
Wimbledon Doubles—1964 (with Lesley Turner); 1969 (with Judy Tegart Dalton)
Wimbledon Mixed Doubles—1963, 1965, 1966, 1968 (with Ken Fletcher)
British Hard Court Singles—1969, 1970, 1971
Australian Singles—1960, 1961, 1962, 1963, 1964, 1965, 1966, 1969, 1970, 1971
Australian Doubles—1961 (with M. Reitano); 1962, 1963 (with Robyn Ebbern); 1965 (with Lesley Turner); 1969, 1970 (with Judy Tegart Dalton); 1971 (with Evonne Goolagong)
Australian Mixed Doubles—1963, 1964 (with Ken Fletcher)
French Singles—1962, 1964, 1969, 1970, 1973
French Doubles—1964, 1965 (with Lesley Turner); 1966 (with Judy Tegart Dalton)
French Mixed Doubles—1963, 1964, 1965 (with Ken Fletcher); 1969 (with Marty Riessen)
South African Singles—1968, 1970, 1971
Italian Singles—1962, 1963, 1964
Italian Doubles—1963 (with Robyn Ebbern); 1964 (with Lesley Turner); 1968 (with Virginia Wade)
Italian Mixed Doubles—1961 (with Roy Emerson); 1964 (with John Newcombe); 1968 (with Marty Riessen)
German Singles—1964, 1965, 1966
German Doubles—1964 (with Lesley Turner); 1965, 1966 (with Ann Hayden Jones)
German Mixed Doubles—1965 (with Neale Fraser); 1966 (with John Newcombe)
Canadian Singles—1970
Canadian Doubles—1970 (with Rosemary Casals)

WONDER WOMAN:
Billie Jean King

When you talk about Billie Jean King, where do you begin?

There's the long list of tournament victories, including the five Wimbledon championships and two U.S. Open titles. There's the fact that she's been ranked No. 1 in the United States no less than seven times, evidence of both her excellence and consistency. And Billie Jean was the first woman athlete in the world to earn more than $100,000 in prize money in a single year, a feat she accomplished in 1971—for the first time.

But the Billie Jean King story transcends her countless triumphs on the tennis court, her eminence in the rankings, and mere money. That women tennis professionals are now fully accepted by tournament promoters, the press, and the public is more the result of Billie Jean's efforts than any other single factor. It was she who, almost singlehandedly, led women's tennis out of the Dark Ages.

There's more. For many millions of American women, Billie Jean is the Lord High Priestess of Feminism, rated right up there with Gloria Steinem, or any other women's lib leader you care to name. Billie Jean attained her primacy on the evening of September 20, 1973, at the Houston Astrodome, where in the space of two hours and five minutes,

Billie Jean King

she routed Bad Bobby Riggs in what was referred to as "The Super Bowl of the Sexes."

Of thirty-two sportswriters polled just before the King-Riggs match, twenty-two predicted that Riggs would win. What they didn't realize was that Billie Jean was—and is—capable of beating all but a very few of the world's males. She strikes out at opponents in much the same way she attacked the tennis establishment all those years, pouncing quickly and violently at the first sign of a weakness.

Not only can she bury an opponent by playing a "man's" serve-and-volley game, she can also, if the situation demands, stroke with a delicate touch, hitting soft drops or feathery lobs. And any time she gets her racket on the ball, it doesn't just go back over the net; she puts it some place.

She never stops varying the pace and spin of shots off her forehand. She herself says that her strongest shot is her backhand, which she can hit flat or with underspin or topspin. It's generally acknowledged that her backhand down the line is about the best in the game. She's agile and quick, her footwork beautifully controlled.

But when you go out onto the court against Billie Jean, you're facing more than a technician. Once the match begins, she scraps and claws, using any edge she can find. It may involve taking an extra few seconds of rest during a changeover. It can be a quick serve or a quarrel with a linesman over a call. It can be her stream of chatter. There's never a

Launching an attack

35

moment that you don't have your hands full. And if she should fall behind, she just fights harder.

As this suggests, the word "choke" is not in Billie Jean's vocabulary. She *loves* pressure. "The bigger the match," she says, "the better I play."

The late Maureen Connolly once spoke of Billie Jean's ability to deal with pressure. "What she has," said Maureen, "is the rare ability to rise to the necessary pressure threshold and stay there for the big ones—those moments when it's 30-all and you've missed the first serve and have to get the second one in. Billie Jean can get it in. She gets to that finely honed point, all tuned up like a Ferrari, and she can play at that level as long as it's necessary."

Much of Billie Jean's success undoubtedly stems from her unabashed love of tennis. "The first day I hit a tennis ball, I knew what I wanted," she once said. "It has made my life.

"Winning isn't all that big a deal. The real joy comes from the very thing that involves people in sport in the first place, the absolute thrill and sensation that comes from hitting the ball just right."

The world's most famous women's athlete was born on November 22, 1942, in Long Beach, California, where her father, William J. Moffitt, who likes to be called Bill, drove a pumper for the Long Beach Fire Department. Both of her parents were interested in sports. Her younger brother, Randy, joined the San Francisco Giants as a pitcher in 1973.

As a youngster, Billie Jean was a shortstop for a girls' softball team. Her father once recalled that at fire department picnics the men always wanted Billie Jean to play shortstop or third base. Although Billie liked softball, she wanted, as she has said, "to be in a sport where she could be considered a lady." She asked her parents what she could do.

Her father told her that there were three sports suitable for girls—golf, swimming, and tennis. Golf held no appeal for her; it was too slow a game. And swimming was out because she didn't want to spend all day in a pool. "What's tennis?" she asked.

It didn't take long for her to find out. Her father enrolled her in a city tennis program. "There was no stopping her after that," says Mr. Moffitt. She went from clinic to clinic around the city. Every time the instructor would look up, Billie Jean would be there.

Her father made her pay for her first racket with money she earned by doing odd jobs around the neighborhood. She kept a glass jar in a kitchen cupboard, and as soon as it contained eight dollars she made her purchase.

Billie Jean played her first important match at the age of eleven, defeating a University of California junior, 6-3, 6-4. The following year she won a Long Beach women's "B" championship.

Tennis became her whole life. She practically lived on the courts during summer vacation, and once school began in the fall she could hardly wait for the final bell each day. "I was usually halfway to the

Billie Jean King in action

tennis courts by the time the bell stopped ringing," she has said. Weekends were spent in practice sessions or traveling to tournaments with her parents.

There was little time to participate in student activities at school, even less time for dating.

Looking back, she says that she "missed a great deal."

It was during these years that Billie Jean, the fireman's daughter, the public-courts player, had her first brush with the staid, stuffy world of amateur tennis. One incident stands out in her memory. She was eleven and playing in a Southern California sectional tournament at the Los Angeles Tennis Club. After the match, the girls assembled for a group picture. Just before the camera shutter snapped, an official pointed to Billie Jean and said, "Not you! You can't be in the picture because you're not dressed properly."

Billie Jean was wearing what she always wore, white shorts and a white T-shirt. But the official wanted her wearing a tennis dress. Billie Jean couldn't understand why what she wore was more important than how she played. "That turned me upside down," she says.

If Billie Jean dressed like a boy, she also played like one. Unlike the other girls who were content to stay at the base line and hit the ball on the bounce, Billie Jean liked to charge to the net and hit the ball on the fly. But her aggressive, hard-hitting style was ineffective against the "backcourters" she faced. They simply waited for her to make a mistake, and they usually didn't have to wait very long.

Once Billie Jean learned to control the ball, things were different. The kids who were able to beat her at thirteen and fourteen fell victim to her bold net game at eighteen and nineteen. "I never won a major junior tournament in my life," she once said, "and I'm thankful for it."

As a teen-ager, Billie Jean had such nicknames as "Little Miss Moffitt" and "Jilly Bean." She had short brown hair, a million freckles, and wore harlequin glasses. At 5-foot-6, 140 pounds, she was not exactly fat, but no one would ever call her svelte. She had a terrible fondness for ice cream and candy bars, and on her first trip east, playing the grass-court circuit, she gained twenty pounds. When she got back to Long Beach her friends hardly recognized her. That fall she walked to school each morning—four miles —as part of her effort to lose weight.

A coach who helped Billie Jean must be mentioned. His name is Frank Brennan. They first met in 1959 when Billie Jean was competing in the eastern grass-court championships at the Orange (New Jersey) Lawn Tennis Club. Hardly anyone there knew who she was.

Brennan, who had been teaching tennis for some twenty years, recalls Billie Jean as a "fat little kid" who banged the ball with the style and confidence of a veteran. She lost in the finals to Maria Bueno of Brazil, later a winner at Wimbledon. After the match, Brennan spoke to her.

"Don't let this match get you down," he said. "I think you're going to be a great player."

Then Brennan noticed her rackets and his brow wrinkled. "How come you use nylon instead of gut?" he asked.

"Would you believe it?" she answered. "I can't afford gut."

"I'll send you all the gut you need," he said.

Brennan later became her teacher. When Billie Jean competed in the New York area, she would often stay at Brennan's home in New Jersey, with his wife and their ten children.

In 1960, Billie Jean gained the finals of the National Girls 18-and-Under Championships, but lost to Karen Hantze. That same year Billie Jean received special instruction from Alice Marble, the great tennis star of the 1930s and 1940s. "She was so crazy about tennis that I had to lock her in her room to make her study."

Billie Jean made her first trip to Wimbledon in 1961. Although she was beaten in an early round in the women's singles competition, she teamed with the eighteen-year-old Miss Hantze to win the women's doubles title. They were the youngest team ever to win the crown.

The following year Billie Jean startled the world of tennis by defeating defending champion Margaret Smith (later Margaret Smith Court) in the second round at Wimbledon. She overcame the tall, powerful Australian woman with what *The New York Times* called "extraordinary display of grit and nerve." At one point, Billie Jean was on the brink of elimination. Margaret led in the third set, 5-3, 30-15, and was serving. Billie Jean recalls talking to herself and saying something like, "If you're gonna do anything, you'd better do it now." What she did was send a backhand flashing down the line, a shot that led to a service break.

Three games later Billie Jean's guttiness saved her again. Serving for the match at 6-5, 40-love, she double-faulted. "When I went back to serve, I believe my knees were actually knocking," she remembers. Her first serve was good, and she answered Margaret's return with an artful backhand volley down the line to win the point and match.

Billie Jean later lost in the quarterfinals. The next year she fought her way into the finals at Wimbledon, but then lost to Margaret Smith.

This was a frustrating period in Billie Jean's life. She was a college student by this time, attending what is now California State College in Los Angeles. She loved being in school. She enjoyed her fellow students, her teachers, and the hours spent reading (one of her favorite pastimes). She had met a handsome blond law student named Larry King, and they planned to be married (and would be in September, 1965). But because of her commitment to tennis, she could be only a part-time student and her grades suffered. On the other hand, because of her responsibilities as a student, she could be only a part-time tennis player, and this was hurting her advancement.

Billie Jean knew it was time to make a decision. And she did. One September day in 1964, she crated up her school books, bade good-bye to Larry and her family, and headed to Australia for three months of intensive coaching and training. "I'm leaving to become the No. 1 player in the world," she told her family and friends. "I can't do that and go to school at the same time."

Once she arrived in Australia, she began working eight rigorous hours a day under Mervyn Rose, a one-time Australian Davis Cup player. He showed Billie Jean how to get more slice into her serve and put greater topspin on her forehand drives. He helped to make her more of a thinking player. She jogged, sprinted, and spent long hours volleying with Roy Emerson, Australia's best player at the time. At the end of each day, she would fall into bed exhausted.

There were many discouraging moments. With her new serving style, she double-faulted frequently. "Go back to your old game," people would tell her. But Billie Jean was convinced that Rose's theories were right, and she stayed with them.

The results of her schooling and training were apparent the next year. In the early months of 1965, she did not lose a match to any American girl. The big test came late in the summer at Forest Hills. There she faced Margaret Smith in the finals. Billie Jean surged to 5-3 leads in both sets—but lost. It was no tragedy, however. After their match, Margaret

Billie Jean gets down low to the ball better than anyone.

told Billie Jean that she was the best player she had ever faced.

"Right then," Billie Jean says, "I knew I had it."

For the next three years, Billie Jean was undeniably the queen of tennis. She began 1966 by winning the singles, doubles, and mixed doubles championships in the USLTA's indoor competition. She won the South African Open, defeating Margaret Smith. She won at Wimbledon, beating Maria Bueno, 6-3, 3-6, and 6-1. She played on the Wightman Cup team, leading the American women to a win over the British women's team.

One of her rare dismal days that season came at Forest Hills. In December of the previous year, the national ranking committee of the USLTA had named Billie Jean No. 1 among the women. But the recommendation was never confirmed by the organization's executive committee. Instead, Billie Jean was made to share the No. 1 ranking with Nancy Richey.

Miss Richey's support came from Al Bumann, president of the Texas Lawn Tennis Association. He wanted top ranking for Nancy because she had won the National Clay Court championships, a tournament Billie Jean had skipped. The other clay-courters, miffed at Billie Jean's snub, voted with Bumann.

In August, 1966, when Billie Jean walked out onto the court at Forest Hills to face Kerry Melville in a second-round match, and looked up to the raised umpire's chair, she was stunned to see Al Bumann sitting there. Furious, she asked to have Bumann removed. Officials said no. She was never able to settle down, and lost to Kerry Melville in straight sets, 6-1, 6-2.

No wonder Billie Jean has been critical of the tournament at Forest Hills and the people who run it. "The one place I hate is Forest Hills," she once told *Sports Illustrated*. "The officials—I don't know what it is—they seem to sit back and gloat when you lose, like they want you to lose."

The following year, 1967, Billie Jean successfully defended her Wimbledon title. And she overcame all opposition at Forest Hills, the players as well as the officials, to win there, too. She was again a member of the winning Wightman Cup team.

In 1968 Billie Jean won her first Australian title and her third consecutive Wimbledon championship. Winning three straight titles at Wimbledon was a feat that had been accomplished only four times in the long history of the event. She lost in the finals of the U.S. Open championships at Forest Hills (to Virginia Wade), but she was ranked No. 1 in the world for the third consecutive year.

During these years, Billie Jean also excelled in doubles play, particularly at Wimbledon. She repeated as doubles champion with Karen Hantze Susman in 1962, won with Maria Bueno in 1965, and with Rosemary Casals in 1967 and again in 1968. She won the doubles crown at Forest Hills with Rosie in 1967. Billie Jean lost her No. 1 ranking in

41

It's acknowledged that Billie Jean is the game's best volleyer.

1968 when she was forced to submit to surgery following a knee injury.

Winning, Billie Jean believes, is based on one's ability to play what she has termed "percentage tennis." This involves two things: Hitting shots which have (1) maximum effect and (2) permit her to position herself quickly for the opponent's return. Percentage tennis allows a player to gain control of a match, and once this happens success usually follows.

Billie Jean's experience with Margaret Smith Court is a case in point. The first few times she faced Margaret, Billie Jean, seeking to thwart Margaret's powerful serve-and-volley game, tried to hit winners right away. Otherwise, she figured, Margaret would get to the net and pulverize her. But percentage tennis calls for different strategy. Billie Jean started sending slow, low returns at Margaret's feet, which prevented her from hitting hard in return. Billie Jean would then either go for a winner on the next shot or try to volley.

In other words, Billie Jean first analyzes her opponent's strengths and weakness, then adjusts her own game accordingly. This may mean that the shots she is hitting are not necessarily her best shots, but they are those that allow her to attack quickly and decisively. Of course, all players seek to develop particular strategy for each match. It just happens that Billie Jean is better at it than most of her opponents.

Not only is she an accomplished tactician, Billie Jean is also one of the game's great pressure players.

She thrives on it. "I've always played better under pressure," she says, "even when I was a youngster." She can't explain exactly why. "It's just that I seem to get my adrenalin flowing and my concentration gets better and everything starts working right."

Surely, one reason she adjusts so well to the tension of match play is because of the mental preparation she goes through. In the days before a match, she will think about the kind of court surface she is going to be playing on, the kind of tennis balls that are going to be in use, the crowds and how she expects them to react, the weather—everything. "You can't wait until you get to a place," she says, "and walk out there cold."

She also thinks about the opponent she's going to be playing, but only to a certain extent. "The press is always asking me, 'What do you think about this or that opponent? What are her strengths? What are her weaknesses?' Well, the most important thing to do is to get yourself together first, have your own shots down, be in good shape. Then you can start to worry about your opponent."

Once a match begins, Billie Jean tries to become totally involved in it. As she scrambles about the court, she often berates herself in tones loud enough for spectators to hear. "Keep your eye on the ball, stupid!" she sometimes says. "You've got the touch of an ox!" is another of her favorite expressions. Other times she says, simply, "Nuts!"

Billie Jean's critics used to say that she was not a top-flight player on clay. The tempo of the game is slower on clay than it is on grass or hard-surfaced courts. On clay, you have to be more patient. You cannot go to the net unless you go in behind a near-perfect shot. Clay is best for players who feature a base-line game, players such as Chris Evert or the aforementioned Nancy Richey (now Nancy Richey Gunter).

But Billie Jean felt that she could play well on any surface. "It drives me nuts when people say I can't play on clay," she once remarked. "My main problem is that I don't get to play on it enough." The facts substantiate this. Billie Jean won the Italian Open in 1970, a tournament held on clay courts. She won the German Open the following year, also played on clay. When she won the U.S. Clay Court title in 1971, she became the only woman to have won championships on all four surfaces common to American tennis—grass, clay, cement, and indoor. In truth, Billie Jean could probably play well on a cobblestone street.

By this time, 1971, Billie Jean was a professional, having given up her amateur status in 1968. The hypocrisy of amateur tennis had sickened her. An amateur, says the dictionary, is a person who engages in an athletic activity as a pastime rather than as a profession. The description didn't fit tennis amateurs. They received income in the form of "expenses." Often they would negotiate the amount of expense money they were to get before agreeing

Billie Jean has great power . . .

44

. . . but can also hit with a delicate touch.

to appear in a tournament. Some male players were reluctant to become professionals because it would mean that their income would be reduced. "Shamateurism," the system was called.

Being a woman's professional was no picnic in those days. The bulk of the prize money at virtually all tournaments went to the male players. Billie Jean recalls that when she won the Italian Open in 1970, she received $600. The winner of the men's singles got $7,500. And there was no alternative for the women. Either Billie Jean and her colleagues competed in tournaments such as the Italian Open, or they didn't compete. The result was that they formed their own tournament circuit, supervised by Gladys Heldman. By 1971, the new women's tour was moving in high gear, offering more than $300,000 in prize money. The figure topped the half-million-dollar mark in 1972.

These were busy years for Billie Jean. She entered thirty tournaments in 1971, winning nineteen of them. She traveled up and down the country, promoting the various tournaments, and promoting tennis, in general. If you did not hear of her or women's professional tennis in the early 1970s, you are one of the rare few who did not.

All of the activity seemed to agree with Billie Jean. Besides her successes on the women's circuit, in the U.S. Clay Court championships, and her triumph in the German Open, she also captured the U.S. Indoor Singles, then capped the year with a victory in the U.S. Open at Forest Hills.

When the rankings were announced for 1971, Billie Jean was No. 2. Australia's Evonne Goolagong was ranked ahead of her. Billie Jean felt that she had been slighted. "Look at the record," she said. "I won nineteen major tournaments. Evonne won fourteen, but six of those were weekend tournaments in Australia.

"They should change the award from 'outstanding player' to 'most popular player,' because that's what it is. The way they do it now, it's a joke."

The following year, Billie Jean was the best player in the world—and nobody disputed it. She won all the prestigious tournaments—Wimbledon, the U.S. Open, and the French Open. She almost surely would have scored a Grand Slam if she had gone to Australia and competed there. "At this stage of her career," said Neil Amdur in *World Tennis*, "Billie

Jean seems capable of winning anything she puts her mind to."

One thing that Billie Jean almost always puts her mind to is winning at Wimbledon. "I love Wimbledon," she has said. "It's easy to get inspired at Wimbledon. You know it's the best."

At Wimbledon in 1973, Billie Jean's opponent in the finals was young Chris Evert, making her second appearance there. It was the first all-American final since 1957.

Billie Jean's strategy called for her to abandon her usual serve-and-volley style and play more from the base line, going to the net only when she had forced Chris off balance. She also planned to keep changing the tempo of her shots, mixing up the slice and topspin.

The strategy worked better than Billie Jean could have anticipated. Her ground strokes were crisp and accurate and she struck her volleys hard and deep. The first set lasted only seventeen minutes, Billie Jean winning, 6-0. Later she described it as "the best set I've ever played."

The second was a bit more arduous. Trailing, 2-3, Chris broke Billie Jean with a splendid drop shot that just touched the cord, then held her service to forge ahead, 4-3. The huge crowd came alive and began to urge Chris on.

Chris led after nine games, 5-4, but then her threat began to fade. Billie Jean's perfect low volley made it 5-all, and then she broke her rival with a

46

Billie Jean reacts to a winner and the crowd's cheers.

crosscourt volley that Chris lobbed beyond the base line. Billie Jean then held her service to win the match.

This marked Billie Jean's fifth singles victory at Wimbledon. Only one other woman—Helen Wills Moody—could claim so many. Billie Jean also won her ninth doubles title that year (with Rosemary Casals) and her third mixed doubles crown (with Owen Davidson).

Winning at Wimbledon was not Billie Jean's most notable triumph that year, however, nor did it earn her the biggest headlines. On the floor of Houston's Astrodome on the night of September 20, she met Bobby Riggs in a $100,000 winner-take-all match that rates as the most talked-about, most-watched event in tennis.

After Riggs had humiliated Margaret Court in their much publicized match earlier in the year, Billie Jean fretted for weeks. She felt that Margaret, by her poor showing, had let down all women in general, and women's tennis in particular. When the opportunity to right things was offered her, Billie Jean took it. "Margaret opened the door," said Billie Jean. "It's up to me to close it."

The contracts for the match were signed in July when Billie Jean returned from Wimbledon. They provided for the greatest payday in tennis history. Besides the $100,000 in prize money to the winner, Riggs and Billie Jean were each guaranteed $75,000 for television, radio, and film rights. Thus, the winner would earn at least $175,000. Few athletes have ever received such a sum for one appearance.

At the press conference announcing the match, Riggs tried to taunt Billie Jean. He said that one of his goals was "to keep our women at home, taking care of the babies—where they belong." He declared that after he defeated Billie Jean, "women's lib would be set back twenty years."

"Why, she won't show up for her next match she's so nervous," said Riggs.

If Billie Jean was nervous, she didn't show it. She sneered at Riggs and his remarks. When asked about what strategy she intended to use, all she would say was, "I'll play my game." Then she added, "I'm not Margaret Court. She did nothing right. She couldn't handle the pressure."

In spite of Billie Jean's apparent confidence, few experts gave her much of a chance. It was said that Riggs, with his masterful control, soft serves, and lobs, would set the pace and tempo for the match, just as he had done against Margaret. Billie Jean was said to have problems with this style of play. It was noted that Billie Jean's toughest opponents were Chris Evert, Francoise Durr, and Nancy Richey Gunter, all base-line players like Riggs. Arthur Ashe, one of the best male players, summed up prematch opinion when he said, "Bobby will jerk Billie Jean around so much she will look like a yo-yo."

Day by day, the pressure built. At the U.S. Open at Forest Hills late in August, Billie Jean was the de-

The heat and Julie Heldman beat Billie Jean at Forest Hills in 1973.

48

fending champion. The press followed her everywhere she went, asking her question after question, not so much about her Forest Hills matches, but about the forthcoming match with Riggs.

Billie Jean didn't last very long at Forest Hills. In a third-round match against Julie Heldman, Billie Jean quit. She was trailing, 3-6, 6-4, 4-1, and had lost nine of the last ten games, when she announced she could no longer continue. Some people said it was the heat and humidity that had forced Billie Jean to surrender, and the fact that Miss Heldman had made her run around so much. Others said that she was troubled by a knee injured several weeks before. Still others said that she was beginning to feel the burden of the Riggs' match.

The circus-like atmosphere at the Astrodome on the night of the match was enough to unnerve the most self-possessed of players. A crowd of 30,492 turned out, the largest single attendance ever for a tennis match. Courtside seats cost $100, another record. Some of the spectators wore dress suits or evening gowns. A band blared loud and brassy music, and large banners, the kind usually seen only at baseball or football games, were hung about the stadium. The tradition of tennis was being shaken to its foundations.

Riggs was brought to the stadium in a gold-wheeled rickshaw pulled by six professional models in tight-fitting red and gold outfits. Billie Jean was not to be outdone and she arrived reclining on a gold sedan chair that was held aloft by four muscular college athletes. She stripped off a blue sweat suit to reveal a pastel blue tennis dress with rhinestones and sequins across the shoulders.

Once the match began, Billie Jean was all business. She made it clear right at the start that she was going to sink or swim with her attacking style. Racing to the net at the slightest opportunity, she hit three sharply-angled volleys to win the first game. The crowd cheered her lustily. She could hear screams of "Atta boy, Billie!"

Riggs shrugged. Calling on his repertoire of spins and slices, chops and drops, he evened matters in the next game.

The games went with service until the fifth game when Riggs broke Billie Jean's serve. But Billie Jean had no intention of yielding. She promptly broke Riggs' serve.

This seemed to be a turning point for Billie Jean, and she started jerking Riggs around the court like a puppet on a string. When Riggs hit down the line, Billie Jean was there to cut it off and hit a winner. When Riggs tried to drop-shot her, Billie Jean would race to the net and cuff the ball back beyond his reach. Billie Jean's father was a courtside spectator, and on every point he would almost leap out of his seat. "Go, baby, go!" he kept screaming.

In the tenth game of the first set, with Billie Jean leading, 5-4, she hit a brilliant lunging backhand for the advantage. Riggs was so far out of position he could only stare at it. It must have occurred to Riggs at this point that he was facing an opponent who was unbothered by the pressure. Instead, it seemed to be affecting him, for he double-faulted to lose the set. The women in the big crowd screamed in delight.

While Billie Jean had looked far superior, dominating the net and running Riggs back and forth across the base line, most observers expected Bobby to make a comeback. Not Billie Jean, however. She knew that her backhand, her net game, and her mobility made her superior. Though there were two more sets still to be won, Billie Jean knew she had him.

Riggs' game went steadily downhill. When Billie Jean showed him she could handle his soft serves, often passing him with the returns, Riggs tried serving harder, which resulted in several double-faults and poor serving, in general. And he found himself chasing lobs and lunging in vain for Billie Jean's many and varied volleys. Billie Jean broke Riggs' serve in the first game of the second set and again in the eighth game to win, 6-3.

When the third set began, Billie Jean's supporters were yelling "Bye, bye, Bobbie." Riggs' handlers rubbed ice on his legs, arms, and forehead during changeovers, but even they knew it was only a matter of time.

At deuce in the ninth game of the final set, Riggs double-faulted, and followed by driving a sharp backhand volley into the net. The Battle of the Sexes had gone as far as it could go. Billie Jean King had out-hustled the hustler.

As cheers cascaded down, Billie Jean fired her racket high into the air, then rushed toward her husband at courtside and hugged him. When they brought her the tall winner's trophy, she held it high and smiled radiantly. The crowd kept cheering and cheering, and Billie Jean acknowledged the acclaim with a clenched-fist salute and shouts of "Right on! Right on!"

At the postmatch press conference, there were more than a hundred writers, and as Billie Jean looked about the crowded room she thought back to the Nationals at Forest Hills in 1967. After she had won, only three writers had turned up to talk to her.

Still wearing her blue tennis dress, she sat on a raised platform, smiling and waving to the women writers she knew. "I felt this was the culmination of my career," she said, sipping beer from a paper cup. "Ever since I was eleven years old and couldn't get in a tennis picture because I didn't have a tennis dress, and I thought tennis was a game for only the rich and white, I wanted to change the game."

Then she paused and looked at the throng of writers. "Tonight I think we changed it," she said.

Just as Billie Jean has been good for tennis, so the sport has provided her with many benefits. For one thing, she's a millionaire. Her income in 1973 alone,

Big headlines hailed Billie Jean's win over Bobby Riggs.

counting prize money and what she earned from endorsements (for everything from socks to hair dryers, from tennis shoes to toothpaste), came to approximately $500,000.

But more than the money, she has derived enormous pride from what she's done. Not just all the tournaments she's won, but more the fact that she's helped to introduce tennis to who knows how many millions of Americans. Of the Riggs match, she says:

"There's no telling its long-range impact. More than the win itself, I'm proud of what the match did for tennis." She gets satisfaction, too, from the fact that she is respected for her tennis skills, as many of the women professionals are. Such wasn't always the case.

Billie Jean acknowledges that tennis has enjoyed phenomenal growth in recent years, but she feels that the sport still has a long way to go. She says that it needs more color, more noise, and a better scoring system. "The whispering and silences that go on during a match are absurd," she declares. "Let people yell, scream, shout, boo, do whatever they feel like doing. They've paid their money."

She agrees that more noise would be a problem for the players, at least at the beginning. "But if you're a pro," she says, "you learn to cope."

Billie Jean would like to see players become more demonstrative during matches. She feels that spectators want to see personalities. She herself has been criticized for her lack of court manners, for her glares, grimaces, and loud monologues. She's been known to throw a racket now and then. She admits that she's guilty of occasional outbursts of temper. "I'm not oriented to tennis etiquette," she says.

Billie Jean applauds the best-of-nine-points tiebreaker scoring system introduced experimentally at Forest Hills in 1970 and made permanent the next year. It limits all sets to a maximum of thirteen games, doing away with the monotonous serve-and-volley matches which were once common to grass-court play. But Billie Jean would go further. "Let's score games 1-0, 2-0, and so on," she says. "And a game should be four points, no deuce-ad." This would make for a time limit on matches, she points out, and make scoring easier.

As for her own future, Billie Jean would like to go on competing at Wimbledon for several more years. At the end of 1973, she had seventeen Wimbledon titles, and needed only three more to top the all-time winner, one Elizabeth (Bunny) Ryan. It's one of Billie Jean's goals to surpass Miss Ryan in terms of total Wimbledon championships. Don't bet that she won't.

Billie Jean took on a new challenge in 1974 by signing up to serve as a player-coach of the Philadelphia entry in the World Team Tennis League. "The coaching part is important to me," she said. "I want to find out if I like coaching." Besides Wimbledon and fulfilling her commitment to World Team Tennis, Billie Jean will continue to compete in several tournaments on the women's circuit each year.

And there is much else to do. Billie Jean feels that the struggle isn't over, that women still have to fight to get fair treatment from tennis officials and tournament promoters. She may have won a few battles, but not the war, not by a long shot.

BILLIE JEAN KING: Major Championship Records

U.S. Singles—1967, 1971, 1972
U.S. Doubles—1964 (with Karen Hantze Susman); 1967 (with Rosemary Casals)
U.S. Mixed Doubles—1967 (with Owen Davidson)
U.S. Hard Court Singles—1966
U.S. Hard Court Doubles—1966 (with Rosemary Casals)
U.S. Clay Court Singles—1971
U.S. Clay Court Doubles—1960 (with Darlene Hard); 1971 (with Judy Tegart Dalton)
U.S. Indoor Singles—1966, 1967, 1968, 1971
U.S. Indoor Doubles—1966, 1968, 1971 (with Rosemary Casals)
U.S. Indoor Mixed Doubles—1966, 1967 (with Paul Sullivan)
Wimbledon Singles—1966, 1967, 1968, 1972, 1973
Wimbledon Doubles—1961, 1962 (with Karen Hantze Susman); 1965 (with Maria Bueno); 1967, 1968, 1970, 1971, 1973 (with Rosemary Casals); 1972 (with Betty Stove)
Wimbledon Mixed Doubles—1967, 1971, 1974 (with Owen Davidson)
Australian Singles—1968
Australian Mixed Doubles—1968 (with Dick Crealy)
French Singles—1972
French Doubles—1972 (with Betty Stove)
French Mixed Doubles—1967 (with Owen Davidson); 1970 (with Jean Claude Barclay)
South African Singles—1966, 1967, 1969
South African Doubles—1967 (with Rosemary Casals)
South African Mixed Doubles—1967 (with Owen Davidson)
Italian Singles—1970
Italian Doubles—1970 (with Rosemary Casals)
German Singles—1971

53

CINDERELLA IN SNEAKERS:
Chris Evert

Once upon a time, there was a pretty, graceful girl, warm and lively, with a sun-streaked ponytail and a murderous two-fisted backhand. One day her dad, who was a tennis teacher, said to her, "You can be the best player in the whole world. But you have to work very hard."

And so she did.

She practiced two hours after school, three hours on weekends, and four hours a day during the summer. She didn't go to parties. She hardly ever dated. Anyway, after a while she began to lose interest in things like that. Tennis was all she really cared about.

She got better and better. She beat kids in the neighborhood and her older brother. She started winning important tournaments and one day she beat a world champion.

All the things she ever dreamed of began to come true. She went to faraway places, to Europe and Australia. She earned more money than she knew what to do with.

Then one day she met a handsome young prince. . .

People first took notice of Christine Marie Evert in 1970, when she was fifteen. In October of that year, Australia's Margaret Court, who had just completed her Grand Slam, ventured innocently onto a clay court in Fort Lauderdale, Florida, for a match with her. Playing Chris Evert on clay is like jumping into a pool for a race against Olympic gold-medalist Mark Spitz. It was a sad afternoon for Margaret Court. Chris won, 7-6, 7-6.

Surely Margaret didn't realize it, but that fresh, slightly built teen-ager across the net from her was a tennis veteran. Chris Evert had begun playing tennis at the age of five, hitting a ball against a cement wall while her dad watched.

There was no grand plan to mold Chris into a champion. It so happened that Mr. Evert was tennis director for the city of Fort Lauderdale, and as such he supervised the courts at Holiday Park, a few blocks from the Evert home. Weekends were his busiest time, and so not to be separated from his youngsters—there were four of them, besides Chris—he asked his wife to bring them over to the courts.

Jimmy Evert looks like what a tennis pro is supposed to look like. He wears a white shirt with a little green alligator emblem, white shorts, and white socks. His hair is white, too, contrasting with his deeply tanned face and arms, and there are crinkles on his forehead and about his eyes.

Mr. Evert has been involved in tennis for a very long time. He won the National Indoor junior title in 1940 and later was captain of the tennis team at Notre Dame. He's been a tennis pro in Fort Lauderdale for more than twenty years.

"The kids are stuck with me as a coach," Mr. Evert once said laughingly. "If they want instruction they've got to get it from me."

It's probably one of the best breaks his kids ever got. He not only taught them the various strokes and court tactics and strategy, but he taught them poise, how to control themselves emotionally during a match. They did not call Chris "Little Miss Cool" and "The Ice Maiden" for nothing.

Jimmy Evert also gave his kids a set of values. Tennis is important to the Evert family, very important, but it isn't No. 1. "Marriage and family are more important," Chris has said. "And so is religion —and love."

Neil Amdur, a sports writer for *The New York Times,* one of whose specialties is tennis, has known Jimmy Evert for many years. Amdur previously worked for the Miami *Herald.* He has called Mr. Evert "a beautiful man." Amdur says this: "His kids seem to be able to maintain the balance that's necessary for enjoying the sport . . . while still preserving a sense of family commitment."

The Everts live in a modest ranch-style home in northeast Fort Lauderdale, with Chris and her sister Jeanne, two years younger, sharing one of the three bedrooms. Once Chris had attained national prominence, tourists would stop and look at the house or take photographs of the mailbox which said "The Everts." It was not a difficult house to recognize because crossed tennis rackets of wrought iron were

Chris at Wimbledon in 1972

nailed above the house numbers.

Besides Chris and Jeanne, the Evert youngsters included Drew, John, and Clare. Drew, a year older than Chris, was less dedicated to the game than she was. Nevertheless, at eighteen, he was ranked No. 3 in Florida for his age group. The other boy, John, Chris' junior by seven years, also showed potential. Clare, the youngest family member, used to practice at Holiday Park with a special sawed-off tennis racket.

Sister Jeanne has a bright tennis future, her parents believe. She was, in 1972, ranked No. 16 in the U.S., one of the youngest girls ever to crack the top twenty. Her wins that year included a surprising victory over Rosemary Casals. Often Chris' doubles partner, she advanced to No. 13 in the rankings in 1973.

Discipline has been one of the leading features in the lives of the Evert girls. When Chris was a student at St. Thomas Aquinas High School in Fort Lauderdale, she would get home from school around 2:15 P.M., and half an hour later she would be out on the courts at Holiday Park. Often she and Jeanne would practice together. They'd usually remain on the courts until six or seven o'clock. They went home, had dinner, did their homework, and were in bed by ten or eleven o'clock. On weekends and during school vacations, Chris often practiced five or six hours daily. A relative recalls telephoning the Everts one

Christmas Day and learning that Chris was at the courts working out.

"She's a good worker," Jimmy Evert once said of his daughter. "She knows what she does wrong and she will work as hard as required to improve."

Chris competed in all the national age-group championships. She was runner-up in the 12s and won both the 14s and 16s. In 1970, at the age of fifteen, she reached the quarterfinals of the 18s, but had to default when she was overcome by the heat.

As she rose in the rankings, she began to compete against some of the leading women professionals of the day, with startling results. In the Virginia Slims Masters in St. Petersburg in 1971, Chris displayed poise and assurance far beyond her sixteen years. And she also happened to play errorless tennis, defeating one opponent after another to win the tournament. As an amateur, she had to reject the winner's check of $2,000, but what the tournament did for her confidence was worth any amount you care to name.

That summer she was appointed to the Wightman Cup team, which matches American women against Britain's. Billie Jean King, Rosemary Casals, and Nancy Richey Gunter—the leading players in the U.S.—had declined invitations, which cleared the way for Chris. She thus became the youngest player ever to take part in Wightman Cup competition.

Again she played like a smooth-stroking tennis

A graceful lunge

machine. Under enormous pressure in the tournament's fifth and deciding match, she whipped England's Virginia Wade, 6-1, 6-1. So efficient was she that the match lasted only forty-two minutes.

All of Chris' winning had to lead to bigger things, namely, the U.S. Open at Forest Hills and, later, Wimbledon. She did not merely compete at Forest Hills late in the summer of 1971, she was an absolute sensation there. With her ironclad concentration and fierce ground-strokes (and her ribbons, bows, and pretty dresses), she caused so much comment and excitement that she was said to be spearheading a new and golden era in American tennis.

Aware of her popularity, that is, her drawing power, tournament officials scheduled Chris' matches, even her early-round matches, in the huge stadium instead of the field courts. She made her debut against Germany's Edda Budding. Although the German woman was much more experienced, Chris won handily, allowing her rival only one game. The crowd was delighted.

Chris faced a more redoubtable opponent a day later in the twenty-four-year-old Mary Ann Eisel, the No. 4 ranked American woman. Mary Ann took control at the beginning, hitting her ground strokes with depth and power and volleying almost every time Chris hit short. Chrissie's serve was an obvious weak point in her game, and in the first set Mary Ann broke her to move ahead, 5-4, and she then held her own serve to win.

Chris seemed as composed as ever as the second set began. Occasionally she would shake her head in disappointment as a ball skidded or took a bad bounce on the soft turf, but otherwise she showed no emotion. They played evenly through most of the second set—2-2, 3-3, 4-4—with the huge crowd cheering whenever Chrissie won a point and groaning when she lost one.

At 5-5, Mary Ann broke Chrissie's serve to lead, 6-5, then surged ahead, 40-0. Chris was being tested as she never had before. She responded magnificently, striking two sizzling passing shots, and then she watched as Mary Ann double-faulted. Chris brought the score to 6-all with a whistling crosscourt forehand.

Mary Ann was never the same after that. In the tie-breaker, Chris was in complete control, winning, 5-1. She took the final set, 6-1.

Chris' next victim was Francoise Durr, France's best woman player in more than a decade and a leading money-winner on the American women's circuit. Francoise captured the first set, 6-2, but again Chris reacted with grim determination, hitting her drives with pinpoint accuracy and occasionally lifting a drop shot out of her opponent's reach.

Francoise was a base-line player, too, and in some of their rallies the ball crossed the net as many as fifteen times, the pace and power increasing with each stroke. It was spectacular tennis. The final two sets went to Chrissie, 6-2, 6-2. As she went to the net to shake Francoise's hand, the crowd rose and gave her a standing ovation.

Chris' opponent in the quarterfinals was Lesley

From the base line, few players are Chris' equal.

Hunt, a blond, bright-eyed Australian, twenty-four years old, ranked No. 3 in her country. Lesley had a battle plan—to hit the ball straight up and down the court, thus taking away the angles that Chris used to such advantage. And she also planned to keep Chris off balance by using heavy topspin on the forehand and heavy underspin on the backhand.

The strategy worked—for one set. After losing 4-6, Chris stormed back behind her searing ground strokes to crumble Lesley's defenses and take the second and third sets, 6-2, 6-3. In her first appearance at Forest Hills, Chris had reached the semifinals. She was the youngest player ever to get that far at Forest Hills.

Now she faced Billie Jean King. Billie Jean had dominated the women's tournament circuit that year, had done admirably at Wimbledon, and was rated No. 1 in the U.S. Chris' parents were on hand for the match, and sister Jeanne was there too. The stadium was filled long before the sixteen-year-old Chris walked out onto the stadium court with her twenty-seven-year-old opponent.

The first game was a thriller. Billie Jean jumped off to a 40-0 lead, but Chris fought back to win. Her boldness had the crowd on its feet and screaming. But before the set was very much older, Billie Jean demonstrated that her No. 1 rating was no accident. There were marvelous long rallies that had the spectators oo-ing and aah-ing, but whereas Chris stroked every shot deep, Billie Jean kept varying the length of her drives and testing Chris with changes in pace and spin.

At 3-3, Billie Jean broke Chris' serve and then took command to win the first set, 6-3. The second set saw more of the same. Billie Jean kept Chris off balance by varying her shots, and surged to a 3-0 lead. Again there were long rallies, but Billie Jean maintained control, and with her topspin forehands, her chips and slices, she made the ball do seemingly magical things. Chris held on to win two games, but in the end Billie Jean prevailed, 6-2.

Billie Jean went on to win the tournament the next day, defeating Rosemary Casals, while Chris went back to St. Thomas Aquinas High School. But no one who had seen her would forget her, not only her splendid tennis and poise under fire, but her youthful freshness and femininity.

Much as been said and written about Chris' two-handed backhand. It's a stroke of enormous power and she is very accurate with it, largely because she waits until the last split second to make contact. Her use of it started a trend. Visit any tennis club when juniors are playing and you'll see countless young players clutching the racket with both fists.

The chief advantage of the two-handed backhand is that it enables the wrists and forearms to work together as a unit, so the ball can be struck with greater-than-normal power. The disadvantage is that it limits one's reach. Chris' opponents often attempt to send the ball wide to her backhand, knowing that her range on that side is restricted.

Some people think that the two-handed backhand

A two-hand backhand is Chris' trademark.

originated with Chris, but it didn't. South African Cliff Drysdale, once a finalist at Forest Hills, used the style. The most noted practitioner was Pancho Segura, the colorful Ecuadorian. Segura not only hit two-handed off the backhand side, but he also slammed his forehand strokes in that fashion.

At first, Chris' backhand was her most formidable weapon. Indeed, it was virtually her only weapon. Bit by bit, however, she added to her repertoire. During her junior tennis days, opponents would often try to hit to her forehand, knowing she would eventually hit a poor shot. But she quickly overcame her weakness. She did so by working diligently with her dad and, of course, she also happened to get plenty of forehand practice from her opponents.

In the Wightman Cup matches in 1971, her opponents frequently tried to drop-shot her, but Chris showed she could cover the court well and hit fine placements. No one tries to drop-shot her nowadays.

Volleying used to be a problem for her. (One of her rivals once remarked that, "The only time Chris comes to the net is to shake hands.") This is natural for someone who has learned the game on clay. You have to excel as a retriever and shotmaker on clay; there is much less of a need to go to the net. But once Chris started playing on faster surfaces, she saw the necessity for improving her ability to volley—and did. Today she's much less hesitant about going to the net.

But it is her ground strokes that make her success-ful. She hits them hard. She hits them accurately, disguising where they're going. She hits them deep, very deep. Make a mistake against her and you lose the point. Make very many mistakes and you lose the match. You must play perfect tennis to beat her.

Tennis fans noticed changes in Chris in 1972. There was much less of an emphasis on cuteness and sweetness. The press stopped calling her Chrissie; now she was simply Chris.

In a tournament early in the year in Fort Lauderdale, she glared at one linesman and argued with another. She once slammed her racket to the ground. Asked about it afterward, she said, "The other girls do it. I'll probably do it more from now on."

Billie Jean King was also entered in the tournament, although she probably wished she had skipped it. Chris walloped her, 6-1, 6-0, the worst drubbing that Billie Jean had sustained since she was eleven years old, according to Billie Jean herself.

Chris not only excelled as far as her tennis was concerned, but she was at least Billie Jean's equal in the verbal exchanges that took place on the court. Often during a match, Billie Jean will shout comments to a rival, hoping to break the girl's concentration. Once, after Chris had put away one of Billie Jean's returns, Billie Jean yelled out, "That was a good shot."

"You *know* it!" Chris shot back, and turned and strode briskly into position for her next serve.

After the match was over and Billie Jean had been

. . . but during a match, she's all business.

vanquished, Chris met with the press. She analyzed the match in careful detail, then shrugged and said, "Let's face it, she was never in it." Chris wasn't being conceited. It was an accurate appraisal of how the match had gone. But *Chrissie* Evert would have been more tactful.

There had been physical changes, too. Instead of a cute little girl, she was now a pert young woman. She had grown a full inch and gained almost seven or eight pounds—"all in the right places," noted more than one sportswriter. Her serve had a bit more muscle in it, and often when serving she would let out a loud grunt. "You put more energy in your grunt than in your serve," her father said.

The high point of the year for Chris was her first trip to Wimbledon. She advanced smartly through the early rounds to come face to face with Evonne Goolagong in the semifinals. Almost from the first day that Chris had achieved national prominence, tennis fans had looked forward to this meeting. Evonne was the Australian star who, in 1971 at the age of nineteen, won the Wimbledon title. For days scalpers had been hawking tickets for the match, and the stands were filled to capacity and even beyond. A tremendous ovation greeted Chris and Evonne when they made their entrance.

Evonne began by making Chris forsake the base line by sending her low-bouncing shots to her backhand. But Chris overcame the strategy and captured the set, 6-4. With her status as champion now

Chris' serves used to have a feathery quality.

They're better now.

threatened, Evonne became more aggressive, going to the net at the slightest opportunity and smashing anything that was high and floated. Her serves began to sizzle. She took the second set, 6-3.

The deciding set was pretty much in Chris' control until the ninth game when Evonne, with her greater experience and superior all-around skills, forged into the lead, 5-4. At the same time, Chris' ground strokes began to go awry. The set went to Evonne, 6-4. The match may have been more of a test for Evonne than her cool manner indicated, for in the finals the next day, she was an easy victim for Billie Jean King.

Back in the United States, Chris got some measure of revenge for what happened at Wimbledon when she defeated Evonne in the Bonne Bell (U.S. vs. Australia) Cup matches in Cleveland, and a few weeks later she beat her again in the finals of the National Clay Court singles. After trailing, 0-5, Chris came back to win the first set, 6-3, and she took the second, 7-6. However, Chris didn't feel that she had evened matters. Evonne's victory at Wimbledon carried far greater prestige.

Earlier in the year, Chris had beaten the top professionals in two different Virginia Slims tournaments, one at Fort Lauderdale, the other at Boca Raton, also in Florida. Each time she turned down the prize money in order to be able to maintain her amateur status. In all, Chris rejected more than $40,000 in prize money in 1972.

Not long after Chris celebrated her eighteenth birthday on December 21, 1972, the world rankings were announced. Chris was No. 3, with only Billie Jean King (No. 1) and Nancy Richey Gunter ahead of her.

Chris turned professional in 1973, a stormy year in women's tennis. The women's tournament circuit which had been formed in 1970 under the supervision of Gladys Heldman, was being challenged by the USLTA, which had organized a women's circuit of its own. Chris chose to play with the USLTA, a decision which did not endear her to Billie Jean King, Rosemary Casals, or the other women on the rival tour. But Chris defended her choice, pointing out that the USLTA had said that players on the Virginia Slims tour would be ruled ineligible to compete at Forest Hills and Wimbledon. "I haven't won any big tournaments yet," she said. "Most of the other girls have. It doesn't make any difference to them."

That March, Chris played in her first professional tournament. The scene was Fort Lauderdale. The surface was clay. It was a piece of cake for her. She defeated Virginia Wade in the finals, 6-1, 6-2, winning $10,000, a splendid payday for a teen-ager still three months away from high school graduation.

Chris went on to dominate the USLTA circuit, earning more than $100,000 for the year. But she had her share of frustrating moments. On a European tour, with her mother as her traveling companion, she lost to Margaret Court in the finals of the

Chris at Forest Hills, 1973

French Open, and Evonne Goolagong whipped her soundly in the finals of the Italian Open. She then lost to Billie Jean King in the Wimbledon finals, and the match wasn't even close. Finally, Margaret Court defeated her in their semifinal match at Forest Hills.

Most observers felt that her game needed improvement, that while she was strong enough and steady enough to reach the quarterfinals or semifinals of major tournaments, she lacked the killer serve necessary to win the big prize. She was attacking the net more, but not always successfully, sometimes winning a point, sometimes losing one.

There was increased tension upon her, too. No longer was she regarded as the underdog, no longer always the darling of the crowds. "Now I've got a seeding to live up to," she said. "It's a lot more pressure."

By the next year, 1974, the improvement that Chris' fans had been hoping for was apparent. She was flawless from the baseline, ripped passing shots that clipped the sidelines, and went to the net frequently and without hesitation in winning the Italian Open, her first major international tennis title. She defeated seventeen-year-old Martina Navratilova of Czechoslovakia in the finals.

Two weeks later Chris won the French Open, beating Olga Morozova of Moscow, "her very good friend," as Chris described her, and her new doubles partner. They had teamed to win the women's doubles championships of both Italy and France.

Wimbledon was next. Chris survived a breathtaking struggle against Lesley Hunt in an early match to move easily to the semifinals where she triumphed over Kerry Melville. The other finalist was a familiar face by now, Olga Morozova.

Chris had much respect for Olga. While she had beaten the twenty-four-year-old Russian girl with relative ease in Paris, that match had been on clay. Chris knew Olga to be a much different player on grass.

But the surface never seemed to matter at all. Chris put on a dazzling show. Besides her powerful baseline strokes, Chris displayed a splendid overhead game and volleyed confidently. The match was over in an hour, Chris winning, 6-0, 6-4. At nineteen, Chris became the youngest winner of the Wimbledon women's singles since Maureen Connolly captured the title in 1952 at seventeen.

The next day Chris watched nervously as Jimmy Connors won the men's singles crown. As the whole world knew by this time, Chris and Jimmy were engaged to be married.

They had met at the Queen's Club Tournament in England two years before. Not long after they returned to the United States, Jimmy moved to Florida so that he could see more of her. Known for his flamboyant style that ignites the crowds, twenty-one-year-old Jimmy was one of the best young players in the world, if not *the* best. They planned to be married late in 1974.

How would marriage affect Chris' tennis career? No one knows for sure. But if it ever came to deciding between marriage and tennis, nobody has any doubts which choice Jimmy Evert's daughter would make.

CHRIS EVERT: Major Championship Records

U.S. Clay Court Singles—1972, 1973
Wimbledon Singles—1974
French Singles—1974
French Doubles—1974 (with Olga Morozova)
Italian Singles—1974
Italian Doubles—1974 (with Olga Morozova)
South African Singles—1973

67

TENNIS NATURAL:
Evonne Goolagong

At Wimbledon in 1971, she sang in the dressing room before the final match. She can be down 1-5 in the final set, but she still can't resist saying "Nice shot" to her opponent. She wouldn't think of glaring at an official after a bad call and the idea of throwing a tennis racket has never entered her mind.

These statements can apply only to Australia's Evonne Goolagong, who plays championship tennis as if she were out for "a Sunday hit in the park," as one of her countrymen might put it. Her engaging smile and carefree court manner have captivated tennis audiences in every corner of the globe.

Evonne electrified the tennis world when, in 1971, a few weeks before her twentieth birthday, she won the women's singles title at Wimbledon, defeating Margaret Court. In the years that followed her triumph, she was sometimes characterized for her erratic play. But in terms of crowd appeal, she has consistently held the No. 1 ranking, and only Chris Evert has offered her any challenge in that regard.

If you taught a ballerina how to play tennis, she would undoubtedly move about the court the way Evonne Goolagong does. She is surely the most graceful player, and one of the fastest and most agile.

She is, in tennis parlance, a mover. While Chris Evert will play the base line and wait until after a

Evonne Goolagong

rally has started to attempt a winning shot, a style of play that is common to many women, Evonne is trying for a winner with every swing. "She'll have a crack at anything," is the way Margaret Court has described her style. "She can be down love-40, apparently beaten, and she's still trying to hit winners. She just won't play safe tennis.

"She never lets up trying to hit for the lines or catch you on your wrong foot. The harder you hit the ball to her, the more she likes it. It's best to slow the game up, rather than try to outhit her."

Evonne is well known for her masterful backhand drive, in which she raps the ball down the sidelines with underspin to keep it low. Her backhand cross-court volley is also lethal. When she makes an error, it is likely to be from the forehand side.

One problem with Evonne is her concentration—or lack of it. Against unranked opponents or in matches without great meaning, she suffers occasional mental lapses, missing shots she would ordinarily make, simply because there isn't sufficient challenge. Evonne admits to this failing. "I suppose I could be the best women's tennis player in the world," she says. "But I'm not yet. For me it's more psychological than physical. It's the way I am."

Newspapers in the United States and in Europe have made much of the fact that Evonne's parents are part Aborigine. To be an Australian Aborigine is something like living in the United States and being an American Indian. The Aborigines were the Australian continent's only inhabitants when European white settlers began arriving there some two hundred years ago. Years of slaughter and degradation followed, and those among the Aborigines who managed to survive were robbed of their culture and tribal lands and driven deep into the near-barren interior of the country.

The terrible prejudice that the race has been subjected to is only now beginning to fade. Up until fairly recent times, Aborigines were not permitted to drink at bars. When attending some motion picture theatres, they were made to sit in roped-off areas. It is rare even today for an Aborigine child to be educated beyond the primary school level.

It was against this background that Evonne came to fame. She is one of the small handful of Aborigines ever to have attained prominence, the first ever to compete in championship tennis.

Evonne has been compared to Althea Gibson, the first black American to reach the highest peaks of tennis. In 1957 and 1958, Althea won both the United States and Wimbledon women's singles championships. Brought up in Harlem, she was introduced to the game through paddle tennis, which she played on city streets.

But the similarities between Evonne Goolagong and Althea Gibson are few, if any. Evonne does not look upon herself as a breaker of barriers. Not for a second. She is proud of her race but does not feel a deep Aboriginal identity.

Evonne can be lethal off her backhand . . .

There are good reasons for this. For one thing, the Goolagongs were—and are—the only Aboriginal family in Barellan, where they live, and as such have been fully accepted as equals by the townspeople. Another factor, equally important, is that Evonne was brought up as a member of a white family in a well-to-do suburb of Sydney, Australia's biggest city, with a population about equal to that of Los Angeles.

When Evonne first began to compete in international tournaments, it distressed her that newspapermen were so preoccupied by her color and race. "It's as though all that matters is that I'm Aboriginal," she said. "I'd much rather people know me as a good tennis player rather than as an Aboriginal who plays good tennis."

Once during an interview she told an English reporter that if he asked any more questions about color, she would "point the bone at him," the hex of hexes in Aboriginal terms. If a tribal counsel decides to point the bone at a man, he will die. It has to be one of the most original methods yet devised for dealing with the press.

Here comes Evonne now, an attractive, well-proportioned young woman, easing her way along the crowded footpaths at Forest Hills. She is wearing a pretty, white tennis dress. It is very hot. She has just finished a match and the strain had reddened her sugar-brown face, tousled her curls, and she is perspiring. She wears a red silk kerchief about her neck and carries two metal rackets. She signs an autograph, another, but keeps moving toward the clubhouse as she scrawls her name. "Congratulations!" someone calls out, and she answers with the wonderful smile.

A reporter with a tape recorder slung about his neck and a microphone in one hand joins her. He introduces himself. "Could I talk to you for a couple of minutes?" he asks.

"You'll have to see Mr. Edwards," Evonne answers.

Someone once said that Evonne should have small

cards printed bearing the words, "You'll have to see Mr. Edwards." They would save her a lot of time. *Everyone* has to see Mr. Edwards.

Mr. Edwards is sixty-five-year-old Vic Edwards, Evonne's coach, her business adviser and, indeed, her surrogate father. When she was fourteen, Edwards, by agreement with her parents, took Evonne as his protégé. He has been a dominant force in her life ever since.

. . . but her forehand is not quite so deadly.

Evonne was born in Griffith, in the sweltering wheatlands of New South Wales, about 350 miles west of Sydney. She spent most of her childhood in Barellan, a scruffy little town about thirty miles from Griffith. There is no denying that the area was once very Aboriginal in character. The place names are the evidence. A neighboring town in Moombooldool; Wagga Wagga is to the south, and the area is irrigated by the Murrumbidgee River.

It is in Barellan, a town of about five hundred residents, that Evonne's family lives today. She has three sisters and four brothers—Martin, age eleven, the youngest, and Ian, Jennelle, Gail, Kevin, Larry, and Barbara. Three of the children still live with their parents. Mr. Goolagong, lean and bald, works at a variety of jobs, as a sheepshearer, wheat-grader, fruitpicker, and auto mechanic. Mr. Goolagong is not illiterate, but Evonne's mother is.

Inside the Goolagong home there are framed photographs of Evonne almost everywhere. And where there are no photographs, there are medals, cups, and trophies that Evonne has won. They fill glass cabinets and sit atop the sideboard and mantelpiece.

Evonne goes back to visit her family once or twice a year, her visits lasting two or three days. "She's a good kid," says Mr. Goolagong. "She writes us every week." "Dear Gang" is how Evonne's cards and letters begin.

72

As a child, Evonne "never cared for dolls," her mother says. She much preferred jumping, sprinting, and ball games. When she was five, Evonne began earning pocket change by retrieving balls at the Barellan War Memorial Tennis Club. The game fascinated her and she began spending all her time at the courts, sometimes borrowing a racket for a game after the club members had finished for the day.

When Evonne was six, an aunt presented her with a tennis racket. "I used to sleep with the racket," she says. "Then one day one of my sisters burnt it. I cried for days."

The president of the club, W. C. Kurtzman, gave her another. He had become impressed with her dedication and began to teach her some of the game's finer points. Once he gave her a discarded net and told her to practice on the flat ground near her home. Later, as Evonne improved, Kurtzman raised funds to pay her fare to Sydney and other places so that she could compete in junior tournaments.

When a tennis clinic operated by Vic Edwards announced plans to tour the area, Kurtzman enrolled Evonne for lessons. This was in 1961; Evonne had not yet reached her tenth birthday.

Edwards was then—and is now—one of Australia's most noted tennis instructors, with more than four thousand players, most of them between the ages of eight and eighteen, attending his sixteen schools. A tall man, his face brown and leathered from years spent on sun-drenched tennis courts,

Edwards also conducts classes at many schools and colleges. His star pupils include John Newcombe, who won at Wimbledon, and Fred Stolle, a champion at Forest Hills.

When Edwards' traveling clinic reached Barellan, Colin Swan, one of the instructors, took one look at Evonne and knew that he had stumbled on a potential champion. "She just flowed around the court," he later told Harry Gordon, a Melbourne newspaper editor, as quoted in *The New York Times*. "She was the kind of natural you see once in a long time. She didn't know how to make her shots, of course, but she was always there, in the right place, without ever thinking about it."

That night Swan called Edwards in Sydney and told him of his "find." When Edwards drove to Barellan to see Evonne play, he was, like everyone else, very much impressed.

At their first meeting, Evonne hardly spoke. Her shyness in those days was such that she would often bow her head when being addressed by an adult.

Edwards told her to practice with her brother, Larry, who was two years older than Evonne, as often as she could. He said that he would come back the next year to see how she was doing. "I wanted to see whether she'd keep at it," Edwards once recalled. "So often it's just a passing interest."

In the year that followed, Kurtzman arranged matches for Evonne against many of the older members of the club. Once when she was ten, Kurtzman entered Evonne in a tournament in nearby Narran-dera. When they arrived, Kurtzman was embar-rassed to find that it was not a junior tournament, but for adults. He let her play anyway—and she ended up winning the women's singles.

When Edwards returned to Barellan, he was ex-cited to find that Evonne's interest had not waned and that her talents had matured. He made arrangements for Evonne to spend the long summer vacation—in Australia, from Christmas into February—at his home in the Sydney suburb of Roseville, so that she could begin receiving intense instruction. Her travel-ing expenses and summer clothes were paid for by the people of Barellan.

Evonne's most impressive quality was, according to Edwards, her gracefulness, her fluid speed. "And she could hit the ball really hard, right at the center of the bat," he said. "She had one homemade shot, a backhand volley, and it was a beauty." Edwards didn't plan to do anything to change Evonne's style, only build around it.

One failing that she had, as Edwards saw it, was her sympathetic attitude toward her opponents. When a beaten opponent began to cry, Evonne would embrace her and try to comfort her, and maybe cry a little herself. But Evonne's gentle disposition didn't seem to hinder her development. At thirteen she attracted nationwide attention by winning the under-15 championships of New South Wales. Some observ-ers now began to compare Evonne with Margaret

In grace and elegance, Evonne holds No. 1 ranking.

Smith (now Mrs. Margaret Court), who two years before had become the first Australian woman ever to win the Wimbledon singles title.

Edwards had not the slightest doubt now that Evonne had the potential to become an international champion. But he knew that in order for her to realize that potential, she would have to work even harder. When Evonne was fourteen, Edwards and his wife, Eva, the parents of five children, asked Mr. and Mrs. Goolagong to allow Evonne to come and live with them permanently. The Goolagongs agreed, knowing that such a decision would be in their daughter's best interest. Eventually, Edwards became Evonne's legal guardian.

Edwards did much more than help Evonne in the development of her tennis skills. He gave her the opportunity to grow socially. Some Australian tennis stars of the past had been as well known for their conversational timidity as they were for their crisp stroking ability. Edwards wanted Evonne to feel as much at ease socially as she did on the tennis court.

After Evonne had graduated from Willoughby Girls' High School in Sydney, Edwards enrolled her in a speech course at Trinity College. She also received private elocution instruction, as did Edwards' own daughters. And, on the chance that her tennis career might somehow go awry, Edwards also arranged for her to take a secretarial course at a business school. During most of her early to mid-teen years, Evonne had either a book or tennis racket in

her hand.

Naturally, she belonged to her high school tennis team. Often she played in partnership with Edwards' daughter, Patricia. By the time she was sixteen, Evonne had won all the Australian state junior titles and national junior titles, and Edwards was predicting that she should win Wimbledon by 1974.

Early in 1970, several months before her seventeenth birthday, Evonne was introduced to international competition. Edwards arranged for her to tour the European circuit, to play in twenty-one tournaments in Great Britain, France, Holland, and Germany. She won seven, including the Welsh and Bavarian championships, but perhaps her most notable achievement was her defeat of Rosemary Casals in the third round of the British Hard Court championships. At Wimbledon, however, Evonne was stricken with a bad case of the jitters, and she lost in straight sets to Peaches Bartkowicz in the second round.

By the time Wimbledon came around the next year, 1971, Evonne had improved enormously. She had scored the greatest victory of her young career, defeating Margaret Court in the finals of the Victorian championships in Melbourne. She had kept Margaret off balance with shots into the corners and down the lines. Never once did she hesitate about hitting a winner, even when she seemed to be in desperate straits. Margaret did not take the defeat graciously. "Evonne plays better against the top girls,"

Evonne covers the court beautifully; she's a mover.

she said, "because she has nothing to lose." In the Australian championships just a few weeks later, Evonne was on her way to thrashing Margaret a second time, but she suffered a painful leg cramp in the final set, and Margaret eventually won.

Evonne went on to win the New Zealand and Tasmanian championships (Tasmania being an island state off Australia's southeastern coast) and the French Open, where she beat Margaret Court again. Wimbledon officials, taking note of these and her other achievements, seeded Evonne No. 3.

During the Wimbledon matches, Evonne shared an apartment with Edwards and his wife. They ate in, Mrs. Edwards washing the dishes, Evonne drying. Before each match, Edwards would have Evonne warm up with Tim Warwick, a young Australian. Edwards would watch carefully, giving Evonne suggestions on how to overcome minor flaws and warning her about lapses in concentration.

From her opening serve, she was a Wimbledon favorite. When she made a mistake and the spectators groaned, she would turn to them and smile.

Evonne's attitude was a big asset. Top-flight players often approach one another like opponents in a life-and-death struggle, each eager to devour the other. But Evonne's rivals found her to be cheerful and serene. They relaxed—a fatal error.

Another mistake her opponents made was to seek to exploit Evonne's most apparent weakness, her forehand. In so doing, they spoiled the natural pace

Evonne follows a serve.

77

and rhythm of their own games. And Evonne, one way or another, always managed to execute a return drive or lob. Julie Heldman and Billie Jean King were among Evonne's victims on her way to the finals.

On July 2, 1971, before more than 15,000 spectators, including British Prime Minister Edward Heath, Evonne faced Margaret Court for the Wimbledon title. Margaret had won the championship three times. Few doubted that she was about to win it again.

But almost from the time the two women walked out onto the hallowed center court, the crowd began to scent an upset in the making. Margaret seemed hesitant about charging the net, and when she did move in, taking advantage of Evonne's weak second serve, she would often find herself victimized by a searing crosscourt backhand, an inch over the net, an inch inside the line.

Evonne had Margaret in trouble early, building a 4-0 lead in the first set. But Margaret rallied to win the next three games and went ahead, 40-15 in the eighth game. Then Evonne got rough. Boom went her serves, and when Margaret's return was weak, Evonne would dart to the net to volley sharply. Evonne won, 6-4.

When the second set began, Evonne allowed Margaret to win the first game, but that was all. Her penetrating drives and quick volleys were more than Margaret could cope with. Leading, 4-1, Evonne was down, 15-40, but still managed to win the game. With Margaret serving, Evonne romped to a 40-0 lead. After missing a volley, Evonne scored with a blistering forehand drive to take the set, 6-1. Wimbledon had a new champion.

With the final stroke, Evonne dashed to the net to receive Margaret's congratulations, and after they had shaken hands, Evonne turned to where Vic Edwards and his wife were seated and waved at them and crinkled her nose. Her brown eyes sparkled as she held aloft the ornate silver platter that symbolized the championship. That night she celebrated her triumph by going to a London discothèque with her friends.

Evonne did not compete at Forest Hills following her Wimbledon victory, because Vic Edwards felt the pressure of an American trip would be too great for her. But she did visit South Africa that year, a trip that caused widespread controversy in Australia. The Republic of South Africa maintains an official policy of racial segregation—called apartheid—which is meant to sustain the pre-eminence of the white citizenry. Australian civil rights leaders urged Evonne not to make the trip. John Newfong of the Aborigines' Advancement League declared that Evonne had no moral right to allow her prestige to be used against the interests of her fellow black Australians.

Evonne shrugged off all of this. Vic Edwards had advised her to make the trip, and Evonne would never question a policy of Edwards. Besides, and perhaps a

She has a deft touch at the net.

Tuning up for a match at Forest Hills.

bit ingenuously, she saw her role as simply that of a tennis player, nothing more. "I don't want to talk about apartheid," she told the press not long before her departure. "I'm going to South Africa to play tennis and see the country. That's as far as it goes."

Evonne was stripped of her French and Wimbledon titles in 1972 by Billie Jean King. And in her first appearance at Forest Hills, she was upset by Pam Teeguarden in the third round. The next year she fared much better at Forest Hills, reaching the finals where she faced Margaret Court once more. Throughout most of the match, Evonne had problems with her first serve, and her second was high and puffy—a lollipop. Margaret would pounce upon it and volley home a winner. The huge crowd that jammed every corner of the stadium kept waiting for Evonne to catch fire. But she never did.

Vic Edwards decided against having Evonne play on the Virginia Slims tour. It was said that he wanted tournament promoters to guarantee Evonne a fee whenever she competed in an event. Other tournament performers compete only for whatever prize money they win.

"It makes me mad that he doesn't let her play on the tour," said Wendy Overton, a tour player. "She should use her talent and put it on the line. She should play for prize money, not guarantees."

Edwards did, however, encourage Evonne to sign a contract with the Pittsburgh Triangles of the World Team Tennis league, which began play in 1974. Edwards himself was retained by the team as general manager.

Just as American women like to win at Forest Hills, so it was one of Evonne's most cherished ambitions to win the Australian Open. Three times she reached the finals, only to be defeated each time. She was a finalist once more in 1974, and this time the results were different.

Chris Evert was her opponent. In the first two sets, both women played a base-line game, rocketing long drives back and forth across the net, to the delight of the overflow crowd at Melbourne's Kooyong courts. Evonne won the first set, Chris the second. In the ten-minute break before the final set, Vic Edwards told Evonne she must begin attacking, "Unless you go to the net," he said, "you cannot beat this girl." Then he added, "Evonne, just believe in God, believe in yourself, and believe in me."

Evonne went back out onto the court and overpowered poor Chris, who simply had no way of dealing with her ferocious attacking game. She did not permit Chris to win a single game. The huge crowd gave Evonne a standing ovation that lasted five minutes. Later that day, Evonne captured another national title when, teamed with America's Peggy Michel, she won the women's doubles crown.

Evonne has other interests besides tennis—clothes, parties, and pop music, especially the last named.

She is never far from a record player or transistor radio. Boys? "I haven't had much time to go with them," she said not long before her twenty-first birthday. The idea of going steady was then remote.

Periodically during the year, Edwards recommends that Evonne take a two- or three-week break. She often spends this time at the beach, returning to tennis with a renewed zest for the game.

Many observers believe that Evonne is going to be *the* outstanding women's tennis player in the years just ahead. She is several years younger than Billie Jean King and Margaret Court, an age differential that has already begun to work to her advantage. And it is generally agreed that she has more natural ability than Chris Evert.

Evonne would like to win the U.S. Open. She would like to score a Grand Slam. "But if I don't do these things, I won't cry," she says. "I love tennis, but it isn't that serious." If it should ever happen to become "that serious," watch out.

Evonne reached the finals at Forest Hills in 1973. Here she strokes a volley against Ann Kiyomura in an early-round match.

EVONNE GOOLAGONG: *Major Championship Records*

U.S. Indoor Singles—1973
Wimbledon Singles—1971
Wimbledon Doubles—1974 (with Peggy Michel)
Australian Singles—1974
Australian Doubles—1971 (with Margaret Court); 1974 (with Peggy Michel)
French Singles—1971
Italian Singles—1973
Canadian Singles—1973

83

THE IMP:
Rosemary Casals

Rosemary Casals may stand only 5-feet-2¼, but any time she steps out onto a tennis court, she is a Very Big Girl. She plays a fiery, bouncy brand of tennis, attacking, retrieving, and going all out on her serves and drives. She has a delicate touch on her drop shots and lobs, and can leap sky-high for over-heads.

Rosie is not only skilled in the execution of "every shot in the book," but she has also created a few of her own. She can volley by reaching behind her back and can return a drive from between her legs. Indeed, if it can be done with a tennis ball, Rosie Casals can do it.

Inconsistency used to be a problem for Rosie, but during the early 1970s she began to demonstrate that she was ready to establish herself as the game's best. "I feel like I'm just coming into my own," she said.

A native of San Francisco, Rosemary first started playing tennis in 1957 at the age of nine when her father began taking her and an older sister to the public courts in Golden Gate Park. Mr. Casals had been raised in El Salvador, where he had been a soccer player. After he suffered a broken leg, his doctor told him he would have to give up the game permanently. So he turned to tennis and began schooling

Rosemary Casals means business.

his daughters in the game. "I was good right away," says Rosie. "I can't remember when I couldn't hit the ball."

Mr. Casals was the only coach Rosie had for many years. "I'd rather have him coach me than anyone else," she said in 1966, the first year she began attracting national attention. "I think it's easier for him to tell instinctively when something's wrong with my game."

Having learned the game on the fast cement courts of Golden Gate Park, Rosie was an attacker from the start, and her explosive style, plus her deftness, carried her to one junior title after another. She won the USLTA's Hard Court singles championship for girls 13-and-Under in 1961, and she won the 14-and-Under crown in 1962, the first year the tournament was held. She won the 18-and-Under title twice, in 1964 and 1965, and she also won the Women's Hard Court singles title in 1965.

At seventeen, the acrobatic Rosemary was a semifinalist at Forest Hills, where she dueled Maria Bueno in a sizzling three-set match that had the crowd on its feet and cheering. At Wimbledon the next spring, the British press hailed Rosie as the most exciting player of the tournament. She looked less nervous when she walked out onto center court for the first time than did her much more experienced opponent, Ann Jones, who barely managed to beat her.

Harry Hopman, the great Australian coach, after seeing Rosie play as a teen-ager, described her as one of the best juvenile prospects in the world. "She already hits harder and with greater variety than most players," Hopman declared. "If I judge her temperament right, she is going to have the confidence not only to attack courageously and go for the line on passing shots, but also to lob effectively in defense."

Hopman also observed that Rosie was a "tomboy type" and "a little wayward." He predicted that this would help her game, but he added, "She is sure to shock a few officials before she arrives at the top."

Hopman should have gotten an award for his ability as a forecaster. Rosie, along with Billie Jean King, has been one of the leaders in the women's lib movement in women's tennis and, as such, a constant critic of the tennis establishment. "Why shouldn't women get as much prize money as the men?" she asks. "Tennis is a skill. I go out and play every day. I've been playing for more than thirteen years now. I go through the same headaches trying to live and play tennis as the men do. I'm for equal pay for equal play."

Once during the U.S. Open at Forest Hills, Rosie visited the press marquee to proclaim the virtues of women's tennis. One newspaper reporter, defending the male players, said that Rosie was all wet, and he declared that he could prove it by beating her in a match. "Let's go!" Rosie demanded. "For money. I'll bet you $2,000 right now," and she started unzip-

Rosie puts her all into every serve.

ping her racket cover. The reporter paled and said he was only kidding.

Rosie forecast that Billie Jean King would whip Bobby Riggs in their much publicized match. "She's as shrewd and as wise as he is," she said. "Plus, she's a better tennis player."

After Margaret Court had played Riggs and lost, Rosie criticized her for letting herself get "all tense and uptight." Said Rosie, "If she played Riggs the way she plays the girls, he wouldn't have won a game."

Rosie is a feminist all right, but not to the extent that she wants to be categorized as one. "I'd rather be called Ms. than Miss," she says. "But don't label me. I'm my own person. I do what I want."

One of the things she seems to enjoy doing is criticizing the U.S. Open. "Forest Hills is outdated," she says. "The locker room facilities for women are poor. The place is crowded with members. There's never any place to sit down and relax. Players have to stay in Manhattan where it's expensive and commute by crowded subway or railroad or in heavy traffic."

Despite the difficulties, the life of a touring professional appeals to Rosemary. "I'm doing what I love to do," she says. "I feel I'm fortunate. So many people go through life and wonder, 'What do I like? What do I want?' I know what I want."

Thanks to her speed, marvelous reflexes, and ability to volley, lob, and smash, Rosie is one of the finest doubles players in the world. During the years

Rosie is never hesitant about going to the net . . .

... and once she gets there, she knows what to do.

that she teamed with Billie Jean King, the pair was virtually invincible, winning the doubles crown at Wimbledon five times and at Forest Hills twice. But Rosie has won major doubles titles with many different partners. They range in temperament from the courtly Margaret Court, with whom she won the Canadian doubles title in 1970, to Ilie "Nasty" Nastase, her partner in winning the Wimbledon Mixed Doubles the same year.

Billie Jean King, who is almost five years older than Rosemary, was more than merely her frequent doubles partner. She was Rosie's friend, indeed, her closest friend, for many years. And it caused a problem. During the mid- to late 1960s, when Billie Jean was winning just about every tournament in sight and completely dominating the game, Rosie was all but eclipsed by her. Whenever the two opposed each other on the court, Rosie could hardly win a point. One year she played Billie Jean in twelve matches and lost eleven of them.

Rosemary eventually saw the necessity of changing her relationship with Billie Jean and did so. "It's hard to be lumped together with someone," she says today. "I've had to create my own image and I feel I've done it. Billie Jean and I are two different people. I've tried to separate our lives more. I've tried to establish myself as an international player in my own right."

One of Rosie's biggest wins came in 1973, when she claimed the richest prize in the history of women's sport, the $30,000 first prize that went with win-

Rosemary Casals

ning the Family Circle Cup tennis tournament in Sea Pines, South Carolina. The methodical Nancy Richey Gunter was Rosie's opponent in the final match, a nail-biter.

89

Nancy won the first set, Rosie the second. In the third and deciding set, with Nancy leading, 5-4, and serving a 30-love, Rosie turned to the drop shot. In the midst of a long rally, she sent the ball tantalizingly over the net to land on the sideline chalk. She followed with an overhead to make it 30-all. Nancy began coming apart. When she tried rushing the net, Rosie passed her, then broke her with a perfectly placed backhand. Rosie then held her serve to take the lead, 6-5. When she broke Nancy's serve again, she had the set and match.

It was a match in which Rosie displayed great tactical skill. She hit a total of thirty drop shots, a startling number considering that surprise is the essence of success with the drop shot. "I wasn't hitting my ground strokes deep enough," Rosie explained afterward. "So I figured if I hit short, I might get her where I wanted her."

Sea Pines was not the only stop where Rosie fared well. She was a dominant figure on the women's professional tour in 1972 and 1973. In fact, in 1973 only Margaret Court won more prize money than Rosemary Casals did.

Rosie has been a finalist at Forest Hills twice and a semifinalist at Wimbledon three times. Forest Hills she can probably live without, but her greatest ambition is to win a singles title at Wimbledon. It seems only a matter of time until she does so.

"I feel I'm coming into my own," Rosemary says.

ROSEMARY CASALS: Major Championship Records

U.S. Doubles—1967 (with Billie Jean King); 1971 (with Judy Tegart Dalton)
U.S. Hard Court Singles—1965
U.S. Hard Court Doubles—1966 (with Billie Jean King)
U.S. Hard Court Mixed Doubles—1966 (with Ian Crookenden)
U.S. Clay Court Doubles—1970 (with Gail Chanfreau)
U.S. Indoor Doubles—1966, 1968, 1971 (with Billie Jean King)
Wimbledon Doubles—1967, 1968, 1970, 1971, 1973 (with Billie Jean King)
Wimbledon Mixed Doubles—1970 (with Ilie Nastase)
South African Doubles—1967 (with Billie Jean King)
Italian Doubles—1967 (with Lesley Turner); 1970 (with Billie Jean King)
Canadian Doubles—1970 (with Margaret Court); 1971 (with Francoise Durr)

BRITAIN'S BEST:
Virginia Wade

Someone once asked Margaret Court to describe the perfect woman tennis player. She would have to be a person, said Margaret, who could hit a forehand like Nancy Richey Gunter, possess Billie Jean King's backhand and her ability to storm the net, and one who could serve like Virginia Wade. It's a serve of marvelous grace and enormous power, the envy of any woman who has ever curled her fingers around a tennis racket.

A slender, dark-haired British woman with steely blue eyes, Virginia Wade used that serve, fierce ground strokes, and blistering volleys to win the U.S. Open in 1968. She was twenty-three. She has also won the Australian Open, the Italian Open, and several British titles (although never a Wimbledon crown). But because her game is so technically complete, it is often said that she should win much more frequently than she does.

Virginia has superb days, playing unbeatable tennis. But when she is cold, she is very cold, and her record over the years is sprinkled with defeats at the hands of players whose names and careers are quite forgettable.

Virginia confesses to becoming "very nervous" in crucial situations. She starts hitting the ball harder and harder. If her opponent is not overwhelmed by the explosiveness of her attack, then Virginia may blow up completely.

Being British may be part of the problem, she once observed. "That's where the Americans have the advantage over the rest of us," she says. "They do everything in life with confidence. In fact, they're a superconfident race. They expect to win and generally do."

Virginia Wade was born in Bournemouth, about one hundred miles from London on England's south-

Virginia Wade

92

ern coast. She was raised in South Africa, where her father was Archdeacon of the Episcopal church in Durban.

The youngest of four tennis-playing children, it was inevitable that she become attracted to the sport. "My brothers and sisters learned it at school," she says, "and they taught me." Her interest in the game grew in leaps and bounds, and after she returned to England as a sixteen-year-old, she began entering junior tournaments. Although her game at this stage was already beginning to show the technical excellence for which she would be known in later years, she seldom was successful in important junior matches.

One reason for her lack of success was that she had other interests besides tennis. At an age when ranking American players are first beginning to compete at Forest Hills, Virginia was working for a degree in mathematics at the University of Sussex, and she also was devoting much of her time to the piano. So while she may never have won the junior Wimbledon championship or any of the under-21 titles, she earned her degree, with honors, and also became a pianist of note.

Of her degree, she has said, "I will have it to use." She doubts, however, if she could ever become seriously involved with the piano again. "Once you've attained a certain standard," she says, "It becomes disheartening when you try again and cannot produce that standard. It takes a lot of dedication to

Virginia is alert as she awaits opponent's serve.

93

To go with her excellent serve, Virginia has a sound base-line game.

regain your former ability. That's why few tennis players can make a really successful comeback."

Virginia has plenty of evidence as to the difficulty of mixing championship tennis and university studies. When she played for Great Britain in the Wightman Cup matches at Wimbledon in 1966, the two days of the event came at the same time as her final exams. She took some exams, played her matches, and then took more exams.

It's not an experience that she recommends. Leading, 5-3, in the final set, Virginia had the Wightman Cup all but won. All she had to do was hold her service. But the player she was serving to happened to be Nancy Richey, who used her guile and experience to save the day for the United States. Virginia's exam results were something of a disappointment, too. She was hoping for second-class honors; she got only third-class.

Virginia began to fulfill her promise as a tennis player the very next year, 1967. In the final match of the British Hard Court championships, she came face to face with Ann Jones, the undisputed queen of British tennis at the time. Virginia was not awed by her, however, and seized control in the opening set with her aggressive style of play. She was deadly at the net and also able to rally from the base line when she had to. Although Virginia captured the first set, 6-1, the crowd knew she was still a long way from winning the championship, for Ann Jones was a steady, determined player, capable of grinding down

Virginia gets a congratulatory handshake from Russia's Yeugeniya Biryukova following their first-round match at Forest Hills in 1973. Virginia was later eliminated by Margaret Court.

even the very best.

But Virginia continued to fight gamely, and would not permit the champion to break her. Several times it was close, however. With Virginia down, 6-7, 0-30, and serving, she won four spectacular points in a row. Two games later, Ann was at set point again, and again Virginia turned aside the threat. In the next game, Virginia broke Ann's service and then held her own to take the title.

Virginia won the British Hard Court title again the next year. Now all that she required to establish her eminence was a major grass-court championship. It was not long in coming.

At Forest Hills in 1968, Virginia clawed her way into the finals where she faced Billie Jean King, the U.S. Open champion the year before. Virginia knew what Billie Jean was capable of doing. They had opposed each other eight times; Virginia had won only once.

Virginia went on the attack right at the start, serving, volleying, and smashing with all the power and courage she could muster. Billie Jean couldn't seem to settle down against the furious onslaught. Virginia broke the American at 3-3, the final point coming on a beautiful lob that landed right on the base line, sending up a puff of chalk, which, as one observer noted, "should have served as a smoke signal of warning to Billie Jean."

Virginia held her serve the rest of the way to take the set, then broke Billie Jean in the first game of the second set. Virginia was clearly in command now. The only question seemed to be whether she could maintain her furious pace. Her big serve was making heavy demands on her stamina, and her constant running and volleying threatened to tire her.

But when Virginia broke Billie Jean again at 4-2, it seemed to remove any doubts about her faltering. In the last two games, Virginia allowed her opponent only one point. "She played like a champion," a British writer commented. "She looked as though she felt like a champion. She *was* a champion."

Virginia won $6,000 as a reward for her efforts. And she returned home in glittering triumph, the first British player to have won at Forest Hills since 1930, the year that Betty Nuthall won the women's singles there.

From the time Virginia first came to know the difference between a chip and chop, her ambition was to win at Wimbledon. After she had captured the U.S. Open, beating the No. 1 player in the world in the process, most observers felt it would be only a matter of time before she captured the British crown. Not so. Wimbledon has caused Virginia nothing but grief. In twelve years of competition there, the best that she was able to do was reach the quarterfinals, and she did that only once. There always seemed to be some psychological barrier lurking there, one that she could never bring herself to surmount.

Yet Virginia has always managed to do well in most other places. She was a semifinalist at Forest Hills in 1969 and 1970. She captured the Italian Open in 1971 and the Australian Open the following year. In 1973, when the USLTA sponsored a tournament circuit for women players, Virginia signed up. Chris Evert and Evonne Goolagong were supposed to be the featured performers (Billie Jean King, Rosemary Casals, and Margaret Court were members of the rival Virginia Slims tour), but Virginia kept beating one or the other of them. By the time the tour reached New York City, Virginia was the No. 1 seed, not Chris or Evonne.

Virginia's serves boom from her racket. Her ground strokes sizzle. When it comes to playing a forcing game, only Billie Jean King and Margaret Court can rival her. But time and again Virginia has proven vulnerable in major events. Hers is a brilliance that is tarnished by sudden inexplicable flaws.

"Tennis is emotional for me," Virginia once said. "I'd rather play beautiful tennis than win." Nothing could be further from the truth.

Virginia (second from left) has not had good fortune at Wimbledon. Here she and Rosemary Casals (far left) face Judy Tegart Dalton and Francoise Durr in a Wimbledon doubles match.

VIRGINIA WADE: Major Championship Records

U.S. Singles—1968
U.S. Doubles—1969 (with Margaret Court)
British Clay Court Singles—1973
British Hard Court Singles—1967, 1968
Australian Singles—1972
Italian Singles—1971
Italian Doubles—1968 (with Margaret Court); 1971 (with Helga Mastoff)

A LOOK BACK

While it is a matter of fact that women played only a limited role in tennis until very recent times, it is also true that the history of the game is crowded with the names of women who played the game with distinction or made important contributions to its development.

Indeed, no person in the United States has ever played a more significant role in tennis than one Mary Outerbridge. Tennis was unknown in this country when, in the winter of 1874, Miss Outerbridge, a member of a socially-prominent family living on Staten Island, New York, happened to be vacationing in Bermuda. There she saw British army officers, clad in white pants and jackets, batting a ball back and forth across a net on a court that had been laid out on the grassy corner of a cricket field. She watched for hours and once, at the invitation of one of the officers, tried her hand at the game.

When she returned to New York in March that year, she brought with her a parcel containing rackets, balls, and a net. The Outerbridge family belonged to the Staten Island Cricket and Baseball Club, and from club officials Mary received permission to lay out a court on the edge of the cricket field. Unable to induce any of her girl friends to try the game, Miss Outerbridge coaxed her brothers into playing. In the years that followed, other individuals laid claim to originating tennis in the United States, but most historical sources give Mary Outerbridge the credit.

Women's tennis as an identifiable sport first came to prominence in the person of Hazel Hotchkiss. The daughter of a pioneer who drove a covered wagon from Kentucky to California late in the nineteenth century, Hazel was a natural athlete who played all sports, football and baseball included. When the family settled in Berkeley, her parents prevailed upon her to take up tennis.

The one court in Berkeley was seldom available to Hazel, so she had to practice in her backyard, which happened to be covered with gravel. Since it was almost impossible for Hazel and her brothers to play a ball on the bounce, they went to the net and volleyed whenever it was possible. Thus, Hazel learned to excel at this phase of the game. Few other women of the period, the early 1900s, ever learned how to volley. It wasn't considered "ladylike."

Hazel won the first of three consecutive championships at Forest Hills in 1909 and she captured a fourth in 1919. By then she was the wife of George Wightman.

In 1923, Mrs. Wightman donated the silver vase for the first U.S.-Britain women's matches, an event which opened the new stadium of the West Side Tennis Club at Forest Hills in New York City. The trophy came to be known, fittingly, as the Wightman Cup. Competition for the award has continued to this day, with American women usually winning.

Helen Wills, later to become one of the game's all-time greats, teamed with Mrs. Wightman in the first Wightman Cup doubles matches. She once told *The New York Times* what it was like to be Hazel's partner: "Sometimes, I would be inclined not to work hard and she'd say, 'Run, Helen.' And 'Use your head. Think.' Young players often don't think.

"And when I would be staying at someone's home during matches, she would say, 'When you go upstairs, don't clump up. Go up on the balls of your feet, it will help your balance on the court.' "

A list of Hazel's achievements in tennis would fill several pages of any book. She won forty-five national titles in her forty-four years of tournament tennis, the last a seniors championship when she was sixty-eight. She was enshrined in the Tennis Hall of Fame in 1957.

Suzanne Lenglen, a French girl, was another of the first "name" women players. She had an enormous impact upon the game.

Mlle. Lenglen first came to fame in Europe, winning at Wimbledon in 1919 at the age of twenty. In the years that followed, she won the Wimbledon title five more times, the Wimbledon doubles championship (with Elizabeth Ryan) six times, and the French singles championship six times. A small, stocky girl with a sallow complexion, she moved on the court with great ease and style.

Her demanding parents groomed Suzanne to be a champion, insisting that she practice long hours to capitalize on her natural skills. Her father would place a coin on the court and instruct Suzanne to hit it. She became so skilled that she was frequently able to do it five times in a row.

It was not just for her tennis proficiency that Suzanne won headlines. In her first appearance at Wimbledon, she wore a low-cut, one-piece dress of mid-calf length, an outfit considered terribly daring by the tennis world of her day. Skirts of ankle length, corseted waists, and long-sleeved blouses represented the accepted mode of dress.

Americans clamored to see Suzanne and she made two trips to the United States, the first of which was less than successful. At Forest Hills in 1921, Suzanne faced Molla Mallory, who had won the U.S. women's title the year before. Molla won the first set, 6-2.

After losing the first point of the first game of the second set, Suzanne double-faulted, whereupon she walked off the court, claiming she was ill. An international furor followed. Americans claimed Suzanne quit while losing. The rest of the world criticized U.S. tennis officials for making a sick girl play.

Suzanne returned to the United States in 1926 for an exhibition tour. Everywhere she played she drew huge crowds. When the tour ended, the promoter rewarded her with a $25,000 bonus.

The 1920s have been called The Golden Age of Sport. In baseball, Babe Ruth was making headlines. Football had Red Grange; boxing, Jack Dempsey. Women's tennis was reigned over by Helen Wills.

Helen Wills Moody

Known for a hard serve and blazing forehand, and for the determined, impassive expression she wore as she ground down opponents, Miss Wills was called "Little Miss Poker Face."

Her father, Dr. Clarence Wills of Berkeley, California, a club player of average skill, got Helen interested in the game. She played only for the fun of it at first. Not until she was a teen-ager did Helen's father realize her championship potential and arrange for her to receive special instruction.

By the time Helen was fourteen, she was competing with boys her own age and older. At fifteen, only two years after taking up the sport, she won the girls 18-and-Under national championship at Forest Hills.

The next year, 1922, Helen fought her way into the women's final at Forest Hills, only to lose to Molla Mallory, 6-3, 6-1. She went back to California determined to work relentlessly to improve her game. When she returned to Forest Hills in 1923, she shot her way into the finals once more and then scored a convincing win over Mrs. Mallory, 6-2, 6-1.

So began the Helen Wills era in tennis history. From 1923 until 1930, Helen failed to win at Forest Hills only once. She won again in 1931. At Wimbledon she won four consecutive times, beginning in 1927, and also captured the title there in 1932, 1933, 1935, and 1938.

Helen Hull Jacobs, known for quick reflexes and a powerful serve, was a frequent opponent of Helen Wills. The "Battle of the Two Helens" reached a pinnacle in 1935 at Wimbledon. Helen Wills, now Helen Wills Moody, was returning to competition following a back operation and a long period of recuperation. During her absence, Miss Jacobs had supplanted her in the affection and esteem of the galleries.

Mrs. Moody trained diligently for the match,

which has been called one of the most titanic of all time by tennis historians. When Mrs. Moody finally prevailed—6-3, 3-6, 7-5—she cast aside her Miss Poker Face role, tossing her racket high in the air and screaming in delight.

Women's tennis in the years before World War II was dominated by Alice Marble, "The Golden Girl." A farmer's daughter from California, Alice took up tennis at thirteen when her brother bought her a racket as a graduation present. "I think he did it," she once recalled, "because he wanted me to stop playing baseball with the boys."

Ten years later, in 1936, she won the first of her four national championships. She won at Wimbledon in 1939. A brilliant doubles player, she won numerous doubles titles at Wimbledon and Forest Hills with many different partners. American sportswriters voted her the outstanding woman athlete of the year in 1939 and 1940.

A stockily built girl—5-foot-7, 133 pounds—she was known for her thundering serve, as fast as that of some of the men players. She was almost as well known for being one of the first girls to wear shorts at Forest Hills and Wimbledon. The sight of legs and soft skin shocked tennis officials.

Ill health caused Alice to suffer a series of frustrating defeats in 1934 and again in 1936. Her condition was finally diagnosed as tuberculosis. After rest and proper treatment she returned to the courts in 1937. The following year was one of her best. She won the

Alice Marble

U.S. Singles title once more, the final match taking only twenty-two minutes. Alice turned professional in 1940 and participated in a nationwide exhibition tour with other tennis notables.

No book that is at all concerned about women's tennis would be complete without some mention of Gertrude ("Gorgeous Gussie") Moran. Gussie was not the best player of her time and she never won anything at Forest Hills or Wimbledon, but she was a worldwide sensation. The reason: at austere Wimbledon one summer afternoon in 1949, the tall and leggy Gussie appeared on center court wearing provocative lace panties under her short tennis dress. "Nothing's sacred any more," raged her critics, largely the tennis establishment. Teddy Tinling, who designed the costume, was accused of "putting sin and vulgarity into tennis." The controversy lasted for months and months, making Gussie one of the best-known women athletes of the decade.

Gussie Moran gave women's tennis a big lift, no doubt about it. Said *Sport* Magazine in its issue of December, 1950: "Until the advent of Gussie, women's tennis was a comparatively dull, unprofitable enterprise that inspired nothing but yawns from the general sports public." The magazine cited Suzanne Lenglen, Helen Wills, and Alice Marble as "other exciting girl players," then applauded Gussie for "arousing the gallery from its long slumber with a little strategy that won't be found in any tennis manual—sex appeal."

In 1950, Gussie joined a group of tennis barnstormers which included Jack Kramer and Pauline Betz, both of whom had won national titles. But the tour was not noted for its success.

Several women players of note were active during the 1950s. One was Althea Gibson, a tall, rangy girl with a booming serve and slashing style that carried her to victory in both the U.S. and Wimbledon championships in 1957 and again in 1958. Born in South Carolina and brought up in New York's Harlem, she first came to prominence by winning the National Negro Women's Singles title in 1947. Three years later she became the first Negro to appear at Forest Hills.

At Wimbledon in 1957, playing in 100-degree heat, it took Althea only forty-nine minutes to beat Darlene Hard, 6-3, 6-2. She then teamed with Darlene to take the doubles crown. Upon her return to New York, Althea was greeted with an official reception and a ticker-tape parade up Broadway. Althea has remained active in tennis since her years of glory, and today is national director of the Pepsi Cola mobile tennis program.

Before Althea, there was "Little Mo," Maureen Connolly, only 5-foot-4, 130 pounds, but a deadly sharpshooter. She didn't intimidate opponents the way Althea did. Instead, she chopped them into little pieces with her precision stroking and cool, calculating demeanor.

Born in San Diego in 1934, Little Mo became, at fourteen, the youngest junior girls champion in tennis history. And in 1951 she became the youngest player in half a century to win the women's singles at Forest Hills. She repeated at Forest Hills in 1952 and

Althea Gibson

1953, and she won at Wimbledon in 1952, 1953, and 1954. She became, in 1953, the first woman to score a Grand Slam, that is, to capture the Australian, French, Wimbledon, and U.S. titles all in the same year. Incredibly, she was only nineteen at the time.

Maureen Connolly might have become the greatest women's player of all time, but one summer day in

Maureen Connolly

1954, not long after she had won her third consecutive Wimbledon championship, a tragic accident befell her. An accomplished equestrienne, she was out for a leisurely gallop on her favorite horse, Colonel Merryboy. As she rode along a cinder path adjacent to a highway, the horse became frightened by an approaching truck, bolted, and slammed into the truck's side, smashing Maureen's right leg. The leg did not heal properly and Little Mo was never able to resume her career. She died in 1969.

While women of a century ago played tennis, they invariably played a pitty-pat version of the game, gently stroking the ball while anchored firm at the base line. So it was for decades. "A woman's game does not include prolonged training on volleys and fancy strokes that make huge drafts on energy, but rather emphasizes accuracy in placement," wrote Lou Eastwood Anderson in *Tennis for Women* in 1926. "To take the net, play an aggressive volleying game, expend energy on twisting services and spectacular strokes are to incapacitate herself and to limit her possible advancement and ultimate joy in the game."

Thanks to players like Maureen Connolly, Althea Gibson, Alice Marble, Helen Wills, and some others, that kind of thinking has gone the way of the hoopskirt. These women made significant changes in women's tennis and in so doing laid a foundation upon which Billie Jean King and others could build.

SCORING TERMS

Billie Jean King has often said that the scoring system used in tennis is a confusing one, at least for people new to the sport as spectators or for those who have never played the game. Billie Jean is right.

To know how to keep score, and to understand fully the tournament sequences in this book, you have to know the meaning of these terms: *game*, *set*, and *match*.

A *game* in tennis is scored in points. But instead of designating the points one, two, three, and so on, as is the case in other sports, tennis has its own names for points:

- 0 (zero) is called love
- 1st point won by a player is called 15
- 2nd point won by a player is called 30
- 3rd point won by a player is called 40

The first player to win a fourth point wins the *game*. However, if each player wins three points (a score of 40-all), the score is termed *deuce*. After the score is *deuce*, the next point won by a player is called *advantage*. A player has to gain a lead of two points in order to win a *game*.

The first player to win six games wins a *set*, provided she is at least two games ahead of her opponent.

In accordance with this rule, sets sometimes used to go on and on, with neither player able to gain a two-game edge. Set scores such as 12-10 or 14-12 were sometimes recorded. Not any more. In 1970 at the U.S. Open at Forest Hills, a system of breaking ties was introduced. Later adopted by the United States Lawn Tennis Association (USLTA) and the International Lawn Tennis Federation (ILTF), it limits all sets to a maximum of 13 games. Sometimes the tie-breaking sequence is called "sudden death."

It works like this: when the set score reaches 6-all, players compete on a best-of-nine-points basis to break the tie. That is, the first player to win 5 points wins the set (by a score of 7-6).

Player A, the one who ordinarily would be going to serve the thirteenth game, serves the first two points. Player B serves the next two. They then change sides and Player A serves points 5 and 6 (if necessary). Player B then serves the three remaining points (if necessary). The sequence ends as soon as a player wins his fifth point.

A *match* is decided on the basis of victory in a specified number of sets in women's tennis almost always two out of three. That is, the first player to win two sets wins the match.

Summing up:

Remember these terms: game, set, match, and remember them in proper sequence.

Four points are needed to win a game. Points are designated 15, 30, 40, then game. A player must build a lead of at least two points to win a game.

Six games are needed to win a set. A player must build a two-game advantage in order to win.

In women's competition, the first player to win two sets wins the match.

When this red flag flies at Forest Hills, it's a sign that a "sudden-death" tie-breaker is in session.

GLOSSARY

Ace (on service)—A point earned by serving a ball which cannot be returned.

Advantage—A point won by a player after deuce. (See SCORING TERMS)

All—A term used in scoring which means "for each" or "apiece," as in 30-all, 40-all, etc.

Backhand—A stroke executed with the hitting arm and racket across the body.

Base Line—The back line at either end of the court.

Break—(See SERVICE BREAK)

Changeover—The procedure wherein opposing players, at the end of odd-numbered games during a set, change to opposite sides of the net.

Chop—A sliced stroke made by drawing the racket down sharply (in a chopping motion) so as to impart underspin to the ball.

Crosscourt—A shot played diagonally across the court.

Double Fault—Two successive bad serves.

Drop—A stroke which causes the ball to "drop" just over the net; usually played with heavy underspin.

Federation Cup—Award symbolic of victory in worldwide team competition among women.

Forcing Shot—A shot which keeps one's opponent on the defensive.

Game—The unit of scoring next higher than the point. (See SCORING TERMS)

Grand Slam—The winning of the four major championships of tennis in one year. They are: the Australian Open, French Open, All-England Championships (at Wimbledon), and U.S. Open (at Forest Hills).

Ground Strokes—Any stroke used in hitting the ball after it has bounced.

ILTF—International Lawn Tennis Federation, world governing body of amateur tennis.

Linesman—An official of a match whose duty it is to determine whether balls land inside or outside the sidelines and base lines.

Lob—A stroke in which the ball is lofted high and deep into the opponent's court.

Love—A scoring term meaning "zero."

Match—A predetermined number of sets between two opponents; in women's tennis usually two sets out of three. (See SCORING TERMS)

Match Point—A point that decides the match (as well as the game and set).

Open Tennis—Tournaments in which both amateurs and professionals compete.

Overhead—A shot executed when the ball is in the air above one's head.

Pass—To hit a ball beyond an opponent's reach, so that it cannot be returned.

Point—The smallest unit of score. (See SCORING TERMS)

Rally—A prolonged exchange of strokes.

Ranking—A grading of players based on their performance for a given period.

Referee—The official in charge of a match.

Seeding—An arrangement of positions of the better contestants in a tournament which assures that they will not be matched against one another in the early rounds.

Serve—The opening stroke of each point.

Service Break—A game won by the opponent of the server.

Set—The unit of scoring next higher than the game. (See SCORING TERMS)

Set Point—A point that decides the set (as well as the game).

Slam—(See GRAND SLAM)

Slice—A stroke hit in such a way that sidespin is imparted to the ball.

Smash—A hard overhead stroke.

Topspin—Forward spin which is imparted to the ball by starting the racket below ball level and coming up over it.

Underspin—A type of spin imparted to the ball by striking it with a chopping stroke; backspin.

USLTA—United States Lawn Tennis Association, governing body of American tennis.

Volley—A stroke executed by hitting the ball before it touches the ground.

Wightman Cup—Trophy symbolic of victory in the annual U.S.-Britain women's matches.

INDEX